PUBLICATION NUMBER 6
Duke University Commonwealth-Studies Center

Economic Opinion and Policy
in Ceylon

Duke University Commonwealth-Studies Center Publications

Economic Opinion and Policy
in Ceylon

Henry M. Oliver, Jr.

PUBLISHED FOR THE

Duke University Commonwealth-Studies Center

DUKE UNIVERSITY PRESS, DURHAM, N. C.

CAMBRIDGE UNIVERSITY PRESS, LONDON

1957

© 1957, Duke University Press

Cambridge University Press, London, N. W. 1, England

Library of Congress Catalogue Card Number

57-13023

PRINTED IN THE UNITED STATES OF AMERICA

BY THE SEEMAN PRINTERY, INC., DURHAM, N. C.

FOREWORD

The present study is a notable addition to that part of the Duke University Press Commonwealth Series which deals with the politico-economic problems of underdeveloped countries. One of these works, Peter Bauer's *The Economic Study of Underdeveloped Countries*, dealt analytically and empirically with the nature of the problems that confront underdeveloped economies. A second, H. M. Robertson's *South Africa: Economic and Political Aspects*, dealt with, among other things, concrete economic problems of the sort that arise in a multiracial economy in which a large fraction of the population is still in a relatively backward state. A third series of lectures, yet to be delivered, will treat of economic problems encountered in South and Southeast Asia, above all in Malaya and adjacent territories. The present volume has to do, as the title suggests, with aspects of the relatively recent economic experience of Ceylon, like South Africa and Malaya, a member of the Commonwealth. This volume is complemented by yet another, dealing in part with Ceylon, namely, Sir Ivor Jennings's *Commonwealth Problems in Asia*.

Ceylon's present situation and prospect are hardly describable in sanguine terms, given its current rate of population growth, even though per capita income there is somewhat above the level found in most of South and South-East Asia. Ceylon reacquired its independence only in 1948, after being under European rule nearly five centuries. Its civilization is old and hence probably more resistant to change than would be a younger and less integrated culture. Its population of about nine million is not homogeneous, only about seven-tenths being Sinhalese. This population is very dense, even by Asiatic standards, averaging nearly 140 per square kilometer. It is currently growing nearly 3 per cent per year, the death rate having fallen remarkably whilst natality has changed very little. This island is not well equipped with nonagricultural resources. Land in subsistence crops amounts to only about one-fifth of an acre per capita, and a considerable share of the food consumed is imported, even though about seven-tenths of the population still live in rural areas. The acreage under effective cultivation could be increased by half or more, but only at relatively heavy reclamation costs. In recent years there has been some increase in the acreage devoted to food production, but very little change in the area in export crops (i.e., tea, rubber, coconut). Employment for increments in the labor force, about 80,000 per year at present, will have to be found outside agriculture. Establishment of jobs for these potential workers presupposes increase in the number of entrepreneurs, a sufficiently high rate of domestic capital formation, and the importation of required equipment from abroad. The funds wherewith this equipment may be had must be got by selling products abroad for more than is needed to pay for the usual imports and by supplementing this surplus through foreign loans. At present the annual supply of capital from domestic and foreign sources appears to be too small to permit both effective employment of increments in the labor force and a reduction of the number of workers who are presently unemployed or underemployed. While the introduction of contraception could not immediately alleviate this situation, it would begin to make itself felt favorably in little more than a decade.

Ceylon not only is a participant in the Colombo Plan for cooperative economic development in South and South-East Asia: it also put into effect its own economic development plan after the war, and this subsequently was revised and extended. Ceylon was in fact the first country in South and East Asia to launch such a plan. The primary objective of this plan as of the plans of many of the densely populated countries in Asia was to increase employment. It is hoped, however, that per capita income can be made to increase slightly more than 1 per cent per year.

The present volume is a notable contribution to the literature relating to underdeveloped countries, if for no other reason than that it deals with the role of economic opinion in the formulation of economic policy in Ceylon. To the best of my knowledge we do not now have a similar study for any other underdeveloped country. And yet economic opinion is a powerful ingredient in the shaping of economic policy. "Indeed," as Lord Keynes remarked, "the world is ruled by little else" than the "ideas of economists and political philosophers, both when they are right and when they are wrong." Even the "practical men" are usually "the slaves of some defunct economist." Professor Oliver tells us a great deal about the sort of economic opinion that has been expressed in Ceylon, how it developed, what circumstances affected its content and direction, and what sort of impact it had. What he has to say on this score will be of intense interest to social scientists of every category as well as to students of public affairs.

Of especial interest also is Profesor Oliver's account of the role of nationalism in the making of Ceylonese economic policy. So long as economic philosophy was cosmopolitan in character, the economic impact of nationalism tended to be disregarded; and even after its existence had begun to be noticed in the later nineteenth century, the psycho-social influence of nationalism upon economic life and the content of politico-economic welfare continued to be underestimated. Nationalism often prompts nations to give up some of the economies associated with geographic size in exchange for the uncertain fruits of political and cultural autonomy. Ceylon may, in fact, constitute an instance. Nationalism may be a source of *élan*, as the post-1947 experience of India reveals. It may also be a constricting and progress-retarding force, as the term "Balkanization" suggests. The present study furnishes the reader with a picture of nationalism at work. It is to be inferred, furthermore, that this account may serve to illuminate somewhat the economic effects produced by nationalism in other underdeveloped countries with backgrounds similar to that of Ceylon. Ceylon's experience in this respect derives importance also from the fact that it is strategically situated in the Indian Ocean area and that it has cultural and religious ties with a number of countries located in South and South-East Asia.

Professor Oliver was well fitted by training and interest as well as by experience to undertake the present study. Much of his research had been in areas that border on economic theory proper, or had dealt with issues in which the policy component was important. His intellectual interests have always been much more wide-ranging than those one associates with "the typical economist." These qualities become manifest in the interestingly written pages that follow. Readers who finish this study unsated may turn to the appended bibliography for additional matter.

Since the Commonwealth-Studies Center is concerned exclusively with the encouragement of research, specific theories or interpretation of Commonwealth affairs appearing in these publications do not constitute an expression of the view of the Center or of the Carnegie Corporation, which has furnished financial support to the Center. The respective authors of the several publications are responsible for the conclusions expressed in them.

JOSEPH J. SPENGLER

INTRODUCTORY STATEMENT

DURING 1955-56 I spent an academic year (June-April) as Fulbright Lecturer in Economics at the University of Ceylon, located in the Kandyan hill country about 70 miles or three automobile-hours northeast of Colombo. Discussions and reading aroused my interest in Ceylonese economic opinion and policy, especially with respect to economic nationalism, the economic role of the state, and economic development. In the fall of 1956 Professor R. Taylor Cole of the Commonwealth-Studies Center at Duke University kindly invited me to give a lecture on "Nationalist Sentiment and Economic Opinion and Policy in Ceylon" and to submit the longer manuscript, which I had begun, to his committee.

This book is in no sense an exhaustive study of Ceylonese opinion and policy. It does not attempt to reproduce or rival such a volume as the International Bank Mission's *Economic Development of Ceylon* or the Ceylon Planning Secretariat's *Six-Year Programme of Investment*. Its coverage is limited, since it says little about such matters as monetary policy, labor legislation, taxes, and a host of other economic questions. Moreover, with respect to the topics chosen, what I have chiefly attempted to present is a summary and general interpretation, rather than a detailed analysis of the theoretical fine points involved and the probable results of actual and proposed policies. Chapter VI gives only a very sketchy discussion of probable effects upon incomes. Perhaps a more descriptive title would be "A Partial History of Nationalist Economics, Economic Ideology, and Development Policy in Ceylon, 1916-1956, with Interpretations and Reflections by the Author."

Nineteen-sixteen is a good starting point for several reasons. It was the year when the British colonial government began to reconsider land policy and appointed an Industries Commission to study the possibility of manufactures in Ceylon. It was also the year after a series of riots, British repressive acts, and Ceylonese protests which greatly strengthened the nationalist movement. Moreover, a 1916 starting point allows consideration of several different degrees of political independence in Ceylon. With respect to the final year, 1956, I have reasonably complete sources of information only for the first four months, before I left the island. News stories in the *Ceylon News* and the New York *Times* have, however, made possible a few comments on happenings since the People's United Front succeeded the previous regime.

For the record of policy, I have relied chiefly on government publications and newspaper reports, the former for the entire period, the latter for 1955-56. Sources employed in getting a record of opinion deserve further discussion, since opinion is often varied and indefinite. My interpretations of Ceylonese opinion came in part from conversations with faculty colleagues and other Ceylonese, but in greater part from the following literature:

The long series of volumes of legislative debates, Legislative Council, 1916-31; State Council, 1931-47; House of Representatives, 1947-56; Senate, 1947-56: These debates provide a rather comprehensive record of opinion over the forty years. Since Ceylon's legislature has never become very large, the debate which takes place there has included not only general oratory and statements of policy but also the more detailed discussion which in the United States is likely to take place in committee rather than on the floor of the House or the Senate. The would-be historian of opinion is also fortunate in that the legislative bodies have in most years included intellectuals with a propensity to spell out the political and economic philosophies underlying their proposals and objections. Although the legislative debates do not provide a record without substantial gaps, they do provide most of the framework and much of the detail. (In the Legislative and State Councils all remarks were in English, and in the two Houses of Parliament most remarks have been in English. Sinhalese has been frequently employed during the last few years, but I doubt that translation of the Sinhalese speeches would greatly alter the impressions gained from the much more numerous speeches delivered in English. Leaders of all parties spoke in English.)

Other government publications, such as administrative reports, and the reports of committees, commissions, and special advisers: I of course read only a small fraction of the vast quantity of materials of this sort, but believe that the items selected are reasonably representative for the questions studied. The classified bibliography following Chapter VI lists some of the more informative volumes. Before 1931, government reports represented British at least as much as Ceylonese opinion, but in semi-autonomous and free Ceylon the explanations and advice have usually come from Ceylonese. Authors of the reports have included legislators themselves, civil servants, business and professional men, and academic social scientists. The quality and ambitiousness of the reports vary greatly, but as a body the committees', commissions', and advisers' statements are quite helpful in revealing goals, expressing attitudes, and explaining the logic of recommendations.

Academic and semi-academic periodicals, namely the *Ceylon Economic Journal* (1929-46), *Ceylon Economist* (1950-), *University of Ceylon Review* (1943-), *Ceylon Historical Journal* (1951-), and *New Lanka* (1949-). Since Ceylon's social scientists rely heavily upon British and other foreign publications, these journals are much less influential than are their counterparts in most other countries in shaping local thought. They do, however, provide a partial record of faculty and other opinion and often give a systematic presentation of viewpoints expressed more loosely elsewhere.

Nonacademic periodicals, including some dozens of series which Mr. S. A. W. Mottau, Assistant Archivist at the Ceylon Government Archives, generously made available through the loan of his personal index and through the services of his assistants: the Archives staff have tried to build up a complete collection of Ceylonese publications, and the volumes made available were probably fairly inclusive. Economic discussion in these nonacademic periodicals has usually been short and unsystematic, and the periodicals themselves short-lived, as the following list indicates: *Ceylonese National Review* (1916-17), *Young Lanka* (1918-20), *Ceylon Economist* (1919-20), *Nation* (1920), *Island Review* (1926), *Young Lanka* (1930), *Ceylon*

Liberal Gazette (1931-32), *Young Ceylon* (1933-43), *Social Justice* (1937-   ), *New Ceylon* (1938-39), *Resurgent Ceylon* (1939), *Young Writer* (1940-45), *Ceylon Industrial Development* (1941), *Ceylon Industrial and Trade Recorder* (1941-46), *Public Opinion* (1941-47), *Ceylon Tide* (1947-48), *Third Force* (1948-49), *Unionist* (1948-49), *Ceylon Journal of Industry and Commerce* (1952-   ), *Ceylon Commerce* (1953-   ), *Ceylon Mirror* (1954-   ), *Tribune* (1954-   ), *Jana* (1954-   ). (Dates given are those of volumes found at the Archives or elsewhere.) Not many of these could have been widely read, nor could the few Sinhalese and Tamil-language periodicals have circulated widely. The chief contributions which the periodicals make to the record of opinion are to reveal additional viewpoints and to help indicate trends and points of general agreement.

Books and pamphlets: The Archives staff kindly made available some dozens of short books and pamphlets, and the University of Ceylon library and bookstores supplied a few more. The small market has strongly discouraged publication, especially of "learned" volumes, which, within the area of economics, seem to include only a textbook, some descriptive surveys, a revised London thesis, and a few expositions of Marxist, Buddhist, and Catholic teachings. (Several of the professional economists' more ambitious attempts have appeared as government documents.) Most pamphlets have probably had no larger audience than the short-lived periodicals, but, like the periodicals, they help to reveal varieties of opinion held with respect to many topics, such as co-operatives, the "waste lands" ordinances, land reform, plantation labor, distributive justice, tariff protection, irrigation projects, private property, Marxism, and "planning." The Archives' collections indicate that English-language have vastly outnumbered Sinhalese- and Tamil-language pamphlets.

Daily newspapers: Since other periodicals have not been widely read, Colombo's daily newspapers have to some extent taken over the functions of weeklies and monthlies in other countries, running special articles on various economic questions, with the authors ranging from editorial staff to political leaders to university faculty. But since pre-1955 newspapers were available only in Colombo or at the Archives, which were too far away from the campus for easy commuting, and since their reading would have involved more time than

I thought could be profitably spent in this way, I did not read them. This lack probably does not result in a serious gap in the record of opinion. During most years two or three publishing houses controlled all the daily papers, so that editorial opinion was not varied. Also, many of the special articles were reprinted as pamphlets which are available at the university library or the Archives. Daily newspapers currently read were the *Ceylon Daily News, Ceylon Observer, Times of Ceylon,* and *Morning Times.* The *Daily News* and *Observer* are published by one house, the *Times* papers by another; each also publishes Sinhalese- and Tamil-language papers.

Party newspapers: Published by the United National party, Sri Lanka Freedom party (chief unit within the People's United Front), Nava Lanka Sama Samaja party, and Communist party, these weekly newspapers supplemented the party leaders' speeches in the House of Representatives. I did not read pre-1955 issues.

Among the Ceylonese who were quite helpful in the study of opinion and policy were my university colleagues I. D. S. Weerawardana, N. K. Sarkar, F. R. Jayasuriya, I. H. Vanden Driesen, and S. J. Tambiah, as well as Mr. Mottau and others of the Archives staff, E. B. Tisseverasinghe and E. C. S. Paul of the Ministry of Industries, B. B. Das Gupta of the Central Bank of Ceylon, Gamani Corea of the Planning Secretariat, Tarzie Vittachi of the *Ceylon Observer,* N. U. Jayawardena, and numerous university students. Obviously, none of these shares any blame for errors, misinterpretations, or omissions.

HENRY M. OLIVER, JR.

Bloomington, Indiana
February 19, 1957

CONTENTS

Economic Opinion and Policy
in Ceylon

Policy-Makers and the Ceylonese Background

CEYLON'S POLITICAL STATUS has passed through four stages during the last several decades: British absolutism, limited self-government, semiautonomy, and independence.[1] Policy-making on the island thus shifted steadily from that of an externally ruled colony to that of a sovereign state.

THE POLICY-MAKERS

Before 1921 economic policy in Ceylon was entirely British. Colonial governors appointed Ceylonese as members of the Legislative Council, to which they turned for advice and with which they shared their law-making powers. After 1910 Ceylonese voters had the right to elect one or more members; but British colonial officials themselves constituted a Council majority, so that they could override Ceylonese objections without appealing to London or making use of an executive veto. Constitutional changes in the early 1920's introduced a substantial degree of self-rule. London retained the right to impose such laws as it desired, and British officials continued to man all top administrative posts; the Governor was still responsible for the government of the colony. But in 1921 Ceylonese-elected members plus appointees outnumbered British members of the Legislative Council, and by 1924 the elected members alone were a majority. Over the decades the Council had acquired substantial powers with respect to taxing, borrowing, spending, and various other governmental matters, so that the Ceylonese were now in position

---

[1] See I. D. S. and M. I. Weerawardana, *Ceylon and Her Citizens* (Madras: Oxford University Press, 1956), chap. vi; and I. D. S. Weerawardana, *Government and Politics in Ceylon, 1931-1946* (Colombo: Ceylon Research Associates, 1951).

strongly to influence, if not to control, policy. The Governor could overrule them by appealing to London, but he did not often wish to act in this manner.

In 1931 further constitutional change replaced the old system with a largely elected State Council which had the right to select a Board of Ministers from its own ranks. The Ceylonese were now able to initiate and develop most of the island's economic policy. True, the Governor still could veto bills or refer them to London; he also had absolute emergency powers plus continuing control over foreign relations and certain domestic matters. During the depression years and World War II, the British showed that they were still willing to regulate Ceylonese trade and finance; the Governor also put up a constant battle to protect the salaries and pension rights of British civil servants. But with respect to most economic questions the State Council was effectively free, within rather wide limits, to act as it pleased. The Governor preferred usually to co-operate, rather than to oppose or impose legislation.

Complete independence came with the introduction of parliamentary government in 1947 and dominion status in 1948. The only external checks remaining were those that all nations experience: that is, disadvantages arising from various lines of action and the rules of international law.

From 1910 to 1931 the constitutional changes that conferred increasing degrees of self-rule also widened the Ceylonese electorate. Before 1910 only British residents voted. As late as 1924 only about 4 per cent of the population had the right of the ballot; politics was a monopoly of the English-speaking, higher-income classes. The 1931 reform introduced adult suffrage, opening the voting booths to the low-income, poorly educated Sinhalese- and Tamil-speaking masses.

The first few years of Ceylonese independence thus hardly could see an extension, and did see a contraction in the voting lists. Both before and after the reform of 1931 imperial citizenship and local residence, rather than Ceylonese nationality, had been the requirements for the ballot, so that British, Indian, and other Empire nationals were among the electorate. As a result of the adult-suffrage rule hundreds of thousands of recent Indian migrants and their descendants became eligible voters. In 1948 the new Parliament, which had gained the right to distinguish between their fellow Ceylonese and nationals of other Commonwealth countries, exercised this right in a sweeping fashion, disfranchising most residents of British and Indian descent, including a vast number of Indians born in Ceylon.[2] Since the British were only a tiny fraction of the populace, and the 1947-56 Parliaments, like the earlier Legislative and State Councils, included several appointed representatives from their ranks, their disfranchisement was of little significance.[3] The new rules concerning persons of Indian descent, however, disqualified about an eighth of the island's adult population, including the great majority of plantation workers.[4]

The legislators themselves underwent much less drastic change than the electorate during the periods of constitutional reform. Before 1931 the English-speaking, higher-income Ceylonese had monopolized the voting booths as well as the seats in the Legislative Council. After 1931 they lost their first monopoly but retained the second. The State Councils elected in the 1930's did include some members whom bourgeois voters would probably never have chosen—a labor-union official, a few Marxists and semi-Marxists— but these eccentrics were of the English-educated minority. The Parliaments elected in 1947 and 1952 contained an even greater number from the Left, but these too were intellectuals and other well-educated leaders, not direct representatives of the peasants and workers.[5] The election which took place early in 1956 saw the first small break in the monopoly so long held by the English-speaking, higher-income classes. The facts that English-language

[2] The main principle governing Ceylon citizenship is descent, not place of residence or birth. Indian and Pakistani nationals may acquire citizenship by giving satisfactory evidence of long residence and intention to regard Ceylon as the fatherland, but Ceylonese officials have been reluctant to accept the proffered evidence.

[3] Parliament consists of the House of Representatives and the Senate, with the former exercising by far the greater power. The Governor-General, on the advice of the Prime Minister, appoints 6 of the 95 members. In 1947 and 1952 most of the appointees were British; in 1956 they were divided to a greater extent among various minorities, including the British. See I. D. S. Weerawardana, "The Minorities and the Citizenship Act," *Ceylon Historical Journal*, I (Jan., 1952), 242-50.

[4] In 1954 a special act provided for the election of four Indian-Pakistani members during a twelve-year transitional period, but no such members had been selected by 1956.

[5] Many leaders of the semi-Trotskyist Lanka Sama Samaja party came from the island's wealthy planters and professional men.

education was the only available higher education and that English was the sole or principal language of the state made their dominance inevitable.[6]

Indeed, before the election victory of the People's United Front[7] in 1956 political leadership altered little more than in accordance with the passage of time. Those members of the Legislative Council who headed a sort of Opposition to the colonial officials became the leading ministers in the days of the State Council. They and their junior associates took over the cabinet positions in the first two Parliaments.[8] Before the election of 1947 one cannot speak accurately of party politics, since the Ceylonese legislatures consisted of blocs and individuals rather than organized parties, but the loose coalitions which provided most pre-1947 majorities were in a sense early stages of the United National party that ruled Ceylon during its first eight years of independence.[9]

THE BACKGROUND OF POLICY AND OPINION

Throughout the changes of government the Ceylonese economy remained predominantly agricultural, with both peasant and plantation sectors.[10] The former was a heritage from the precolonial,

[6] During the 1950's some members of Parliament delivered their speeches in Sinhalese or Tamil and thus were unintelligible to many of their fellows.

[7] This winning coalition (in Sinhalese the Mahajana Eksath Peramuna) consisted of the semi-socialist Sri Lanka Freedom party and certain groups formerly affiliated with the semi-Trotskyist Lanka Sama Samaja party. See below, chap. iii, pp. 56-60.

[8] The two most prominent names in the independence movement were D. B. Jayatilaka and D. S. Senanayake. Both were active in the Legislative Council and served as Leaders of the State Council, the former until, the latter after, 1942. Senanayake served as Prime Minister from 1947 until his death in 1952, when he was succeeded by his son Dudley Senanayake. J. L. Kotelawala, Prime Minister during 1953-56, was D. S. Senanayake's nephew and leading lieutenant. S. W. R. D. Bandaranaike, who became Prime Minister in 1956, also was active in the nationalist movement of the 1920's and 1930's and served in D. S. Senanayake's post-independence cabinet, but broke with the ruling United National Party in 1951.

[9] A Labor party came into existence in 1920, but remained a minuscule part of Ceylonese political life. The mid-thirties saw the birth of the Lanka Sama Samaja party, which later broke into the Communist party and two semi-Trotskyist segments claiming the original name. Party-like organizations in pre-independence years included the Ceylon National Congress, the Tamil Congress (representing Ceylon Tamils but not Indian Tamils in Ceylon), and the Sinhala Maha Sabha, in some ways a forerunner of the Sinhalese Sri Lanka Freedom party. Various Council members and others believing in an almost Gladstonian Liberalism formed a Liberal League in the early 1930's.

[10] The census of 1946 showed the following occupational distribution: agriculture, forestry, and fishing 53 per cent; industry 11 per cent; trade, transport, and

feudal Ceylon, the latter a product of nineteenth-century British policy;[11] it existed and could exist only as part of an international economy that provided suitable markets for tea, rubber, and coconut derivatives and offered suitable supplies of foodstuffs and various manufactured goods at sufficiently low prices. Directly or indirectly, the plantations also dominated the manufacturing and commerce of the island. Tea and rubber factories, located on the plantations themselves; coconut oil mills, located in plantation areas; and machine shops servicing the plantation establishments provided much of the island's factory employment.[12] Colombo, Ceylon's capital and only important commercial center, served primarily as a transshipment point for the export of goods from and import of goods for the tea-rubber-coconut country, and as a residence for the governmental employees, whose wages mostly came from the revenues provided by the plantation sector's export-import trade.

In colonial Ceylon the British were the economic as well as the political lords of the island. British landlords owned, and British owners or agents managed, most of the large tea and rubber estates; British merchants and bankers were the top commercial figures. The rise of a wealthy Ceylonese class of planters,[13] merchants, and professional men preceded the gaining of semiautonomy; but on the whole the British loss of economic prominence took place much more slowly than the British loss of political power. When Ceylon became an independent dominion in 1948, British capital and management still controlled the bulk of the tea and the greater part of the rubber acreage, plus most of the large-scale business establishments in Colombo. During the subsequent period Ceylonese planters have bought many British estates, and both local capitalists and the

banking 21 per cent; service occupations 15 per cent. Persons gainfully employed on tea, rubber, and coconut plantations were much more numerous than those raising paddy and other crops. Most "industrial" employment was nonfactory.

[11] See I. H. Vanden Driesen, "The History of Coffee Culture in Ceylon," *Ceylon Historical Journal*, III (July, 1953), 31-61.

[12] Census statistics do not show this, since the Ceylonese do not consider tea and rubber factories to be "industrial" establishments. Their employees are grouped together with other plantation workers. The 1952 *Census of Industry* listed 692 establishments employing 53,457 persons.

[13] Ceylonese planters dominated coconut production. Their estates were usually small. In 1946, 58 per cent of the persons gainfully occupied on coconut plantations were self-employed. Some planter families had mining interests as well. D. S. Senanayake, Leader of the State Council and Prime Minister, derived much of his income from plumbago (graphite).

government have developed enterprises, cutting into the percentage of nonagricultural business that is British-owned; but the British are still the economic leaders.

A second foreign group has also played a prominent role in Ceylon's economic life. During the nineteenth century Indian merchants, money-lenders, and laborers began to cross Palk Strait to take advantage of the opportunities appearing in the colony run by India's own masters. The merchants, heirs to a commercial tradition that few Ceylonese shared, became dominant in certain areas of retail trade; the money-lenders specialized in small loans to villagers and other low-income debtors; most of the laborers found work on the British tea and rubber estates and there formed by far the greater part of the labor force.[14]

The Ceylonese population initially played only a small role in the transformation of their economy. This was especially true of the Kandyan, or central highland, area, where the Sinhalese feudal kingdom had lasted until 1815 and Portuguese-Dutch influences had largely been kept away from the small number of landed aristocrats, petty merchants, and Buddhist intellectuals as well as the masses of peasant farmers and village laborers; economic life was dominated by feudal obligations and caste rather than commercial exchange. Even in the coastal lowlands long under European rule, business attitudes and experiences in the early nineteenth century were chiefly restricted to a small number of Burghers,[15] other Christians, and Muslim traders.

By the time of World War I, however, the heirs of the future had made their appearance: a fairly numerous Ceylonese bourgeoisie consisting in part of planters and merchants who followed in British footsteps, sometimes to achieve great wealth; in part of the public servants whom colonial officers trained, initially to take care of minor duties; in part of the lawyers, doctors, academicians, and other intellectuals growing out of the more primary bourgeois groups. The Burgher and other Christian minorities constituted disproportionately high percentages of these ranks, but the island's

[14] Most of the Indians were Tamils and thus spoke the same language as Ceylon's most numerous minority. But most Ceylonese make a sharp distinction between Ceylon Tamils and "Indian" Tamils in Ceylon, who are not considered Ceylonese.

[15] Of partly European ancestry, more usually Dutch, sometimes Portuguese or English.

majority of Sinhalese Buddhists and most numerous minority of Tamil Hindus were substantially represented.

In many, perhaps most, important characteristics the Ceylonese bourgeoisie were a Westernized class. This was especially true of its intellectuals. Their first language was English rather than Sinhalese or Tamil; their social thought came chiefly from British and Continental sources rather than from traditional Ceylonese philosophies and ways of life. The interests and sympathies of the great majority, however, differed widely from those of the British political and economic lords of Ceylon. They were the latter's rivals in the struggle for riches, position, and power, ambitious newcomers who chiefly felt a solidarity of interest among themselves, rather than with the established group whom they hoped to displace. They were Ceylonese—and keenly aware of it in the presence of European racial snobbery. Even the Burghers, who on the whole enjoyed a preferred position under colonial rule, contributed a sizable quota of leaders and workers to the nationalist cause.[16]

The vast majority of Ceylonese remained rural dwellers, with little or no knowledge of English and little schooling. In other respects as well they were only slightly Westernized and thus differed greatly from the educated bourgeoisie.[17] Sinhalese-speakers were predominantly Buddhist, Tamil-speakers were mostly Hindus and Muslims. Authority in the villages was shared by government representatives, wealthy or aristocratic landowners, and the priestly order. In Buddhist communities *bhikkus*[18] enjoyed especially great respect. Caste distinctions survived among both Buddhists and Hindus, although they were much less rigorous among the former.

As improved medical care and other developments reduced the death rate, the rising agricultural population began to suffer from landlessness and underemployment.[19] Scores of thousands moved

[16] See Sir Ivor Jennings, "Nationalism and Political Development in Ceylon," *Ceylon Historical Journal*, III (July, 1953-April, 1954), 62-85, 99-114, 197-206.

[17] See N. D. Wijesekera, *The People of Ceylon* (Colombo: M. D. Gunasena and Co., 1950); Bryce Ryan, *Caste in Modern Ceylon* (New Brunswick, N. J.: Rutgers University Press, 1953); Ralph Pieris, "Society and Ideology in Ceylon during a 'Time of Troubles,' 1795-1850," *University of Ceylon Review*, IX (July-Oct., 1951), 171-85, 266-79, X (Jan., 1952), 79-102.

[18] Members of a monastic order often performing most of the functions associated with priests in other religions.

[19] By 1950 about a quarter of the farm families owned no land, a half owned less than an acre, and two-thirds owned less than two acres. Paddy farmers' holdings

into Colombo and the smaller towns, but the natural increase in the rural areas was much too great for such migration to provide more than partial relief. Agricultural expansion via irrigation in the Dry Zone also took place far too slowly. Debt, foreclosure, and tenancy added to the small farmers' troubles. In the central highlands the steadily decreasing size of holdings and percentage of owner-cultivators intensified the interest with which Sinhalese looked at the British tea and rubber estates, developed from "waste" lands seized and sold by the colonial government during the preceding century,[20] and at the Indian workers who constituted the bulk of the plantations' labor force.[21]

Ceylon's educated youth also experienced their frustrations. After 1947 political independence was complete, and Ceylonese continued slowly to replace British in leading economic posts, but the number of well-paying, white-collar positions available for Ceylonese did not increase as rapidly as the number of young men expecting them. Frustration was widespread even among the English-educated, who discovered that their university degrees and secondary-school certificates frequently did not win for them the governmental and other good jobs which similar education had won for the preceding generation. It apparently was common among the newest group to receive secondary-school education, i.e., thousands of young men and women were educated in Sinhalese or Tamil and were hence unable to compete on even terms for entrance into the English-speaking university, government offices, and professions.[22]

Discontent was especially great among the Sinhalese, who resented the British plantations and Indian laborers in their midst, who did not include nearly as high a percentage of English-speakers, civil servants,

tended to be even smaller. See I. D. S. and M. I. Weerawardana, *op. cit.*, pp. 34-36.
[20] Ceylonese argue that the uncultivated lands then seized were in actuality village reserves akin to the commons enclosed in Tudor England. See Ralph Pieris, *op. cit.*, Jan., 1952; I. H. Vanden Driesen, *op. cit.*; *Report of the Kandyan Peasantry Commission* (Sessional Paper XVIII, 1951), pp. 71-72. Also see below, chap. ii, n. 3.
[21] By 1946 about a fifth of the plantation workers were Sinhalese. The percentage had been lower in earlier years and rose during the subsequent decade.
[22] See G. C. Mendis, "The Causes of Communal Conflict in Ceylon," *University of Ceylon Review*, I (April, 1943), 41-49; G. C. Mendis, "Adult Franchise and Educational Reform," *ibid.*, II (Nov., 1944), 37-44; W. Ivor Jennings, "Race, Religion and Opportunity in the University of Ceylon," *ibid.*, II (Nov., 1944), 1-13; H. A. Passé, "The English Language in Ceylon," *ibid.*, Vol. I (Nov., 1943), 50-65.

and university graduates as the Tamils, and who as the majority population and descendants of the ancient Ceylonese felt that theirs was the right to dominate in Ceylon. By the time of the 1956 election resurgent Sinhalism, with an emphasis on Buddhism[23] and the Sinhalese tongue, was the strongest social and political force in Ceylon.

[23] Buddhists especially dislike and distrust the Christians' disproportionate representation in, and control of, Ceylonese education. A high percentage of Ceylonese schools are church-run, but state-assisted, and a high percentage of young Buddhists attend Christian, state-assisted schools.

2

Nationalism and Economics

NATIONALIST SENTIMENT has pervaded almost all areas of Ceylonese economic thought. Because of the "colonial" nature of their economy, Ceylonese legislators and publicists have been continually aware of the relationships between their people and the governments or nationals of other countries. Because of the colonial or semicolonial nature of their government before 1947, they have placed great stress on the ways in which independence could affect those relationships. Prices of imports and exports, the terms of international trade, have governed the economic life of most of the country; much of the trade has been with the British, Ceylon's imperial masters, whom they must inevitably have suspected of using political power to economic advantage. Britain's role has been even more conspicuous on the island itself, where modern economic development has been very largely a British product, and wealth, economic prominence, and British nationality have been fairly closely correlated. Ceylon's nationals have also been quite conscious of the Indians, who early became a widespread mercantile and money-lending community and the chief source of agricultural labor for British employers. Since World War II many Ceylonese, like others in south Asia, have become conscious of the Americans, whom they suspect of wishing to move in as the British move out, or of seeking political influence and economic control in the area.

In the circumstances, it was inevitable that Ceylonese economic opinion should constantly make a distinction between "us" and "them," between citizens and foreigners, whether the subject under discussion was economic development, economic stability, the distribution of income, property rights, labor legislation, banking, or international trade and finance. Legislators and publicists in other countries stress such a distinction when international relationships are important. It was also inevitable that much Ceylonese opinion should assign a major portion of the country's economic woes to foreign misrule, and entertain roseate hopes about the changes that would come with independence. In this the island's nationalists have repeated the experience of enthusiastic Western democrats who believed that economic miseries were in large part attributable to despotic governments and would quickly vanish in the glad new republican day.

All ranks of Ceylonese politicians and writers, from conservative to Communist, have shared this nationalist emphasis in economic opinion, this constant stressing of the distinction between "us" and "them." Debates among the different parties and groups have often taken the form of asserting one's own and denying one's rivals' nationalism. Those Leftists who have on occasion appeared to depart from the pattern by proclaiming, "We are internationalists!" have at the most been Asianists;[1] they have concentrated heavily on the sins of Western oppressors.

Nationalist sentiment has, indeed, sparked the drive for economic change. Reformers who have wished to distribute income, wealth, and opportunity in a more nearly equal fashion have been nationalists as well as egalitarians. Writers and speakers stressing "development" have defined economic growth in nationalist terms, have looked on rising income and wealth not only as goods in themselves but also as means of assuring Ceylon and the Ceylonese their rightful place in the sun.

A knowledge of nationalist views and emotions is thus essential to an understanding of general economic opinion and policy on the island. The record of Ceylonese economic opinion is in large part the record of nationalist complaints and ambitions.

FOREIGN EXPLOITATION

Much of the nationalist argument has revolved around the concept of foreign exploitation. Ceylonese spokesmen of nearly all

[1] The semi-Trotskyite Lanka Sama Samaja party has fairly consistently talked and acted so as not to distinguish between indigenous Ceylonese and workers of Indian birth or recent descent. "Indians" constitute the great majority of plantation workers and a substantial percentage of the urban proletariat.

political persuasions have frequently and vigorously accused the British and other foreigners of using political and market power to rob the island's inhabitants of property, income, and opportunity. In so far as this general charge is concerned, nationalism and Marxism have largely merged. Differences between the Left and the non-Left relate to the degree of exploitation, its basic causes, and the roles of local capitalists and landlords, rather than to the reality of foreign guilt and Ceylonese injury.[2]

At least until recent years, most charges have been directed against British colonial government and British capitalists. Among varieties of British governmental action which have been denounced as exploitative have been the seizure of property, the redistribution of income via taxes and expenditures, and the imposition of economic controls. Among the sins attributed to British capitalists have been monopoly, discrimination against the Ceylonese, and the employment of aliens. Marxists and some other critics have combined the many charges into an integrated whole, in which British colonial capitalism is the villain.

One of the bitterest accusations is that which relates to the "waste lands" ordinances of the nineteenth century, under which the colonial government took title to vast areas of uncultivated hill land in central Ceylon and sold them to British planters, including some closely associated with the colonial regime.[3] In the eyes of Ceylonese critics, the seizure was legalized theft, since, according to old custom, the uncultivated lands surrounding the villages were reserves akin to the commons of pre-Tudor England. These wooded tracts were continually utilized as pasturage and a source of fuel and also enabled the villages to expand when wasteful farming or a rising population required new acreage.

[2] Non-Marxists have used the words "exploit" and "exploitation" less frequently than the Leftist critics and of course have not accepted the Marxist "surplus value" doctrine.

[3] Ceylonese attacks on the "waste lands" ordinances appear in many volumes of legislative debates. See *Legislative Council, 1923*, pp. 313, 680-81 ff., *1926*, pp. 829, 1467; *1927*, pp. 421-23; *1931*, p. 559; *State Council, 1931*, p. 212; *1932*, pp. 415, 1135; *1941*, p. 545; *1943*, pp. 1387, 1394; *House of Representatives, 1948-49*, vol. 4, col. 1233-34, 1366-67, 1432-33; vol. 5, col. 453-54, *1905*; *1951-52*, vol. 10, col. 1438, 1517-18; vol. 11, col. 713; *1954-55*, vol. 18, col. 1090. Also see Lanka Putra, *Mother Lanka* (Colombo: Ceylon Stationers, Ltd., 1930), pp. 11-12; and D. C. Vijayavardhana, *Revolt in the Temple* (Colombo: Sinha Publications, 1953), p. 108.

Ceylonese resentment was the greater because the tea and rubber estates which grew out of the waste lands ordinances were chiefly a foreign enclave, run by British owners and managers and worked by a labor force imported from south India. The plantations sold their output through British-owned, British-managed export houses and shipping lines, and bought their supplies from British and Indian merchants. To many Ceylonese it looked as though the land seizures were not only an initial act of robbery, but also a source of continuing spoliation as one group of foreigners shipped profits out of the country while another took jobs away from the island's inhabitants.[4]

This hostile attitude towards the British plantations helps to explain a second charge brought against the colonial government, the charge that its taxes and outlays took income away from Ceylonese and gave it to foreigners. Nationalists thought that roads and agricultural research for the tea and rubber estates were much too large a part of the budget,[5] and that British investors and residents paid too small a part of the taxes.[6] But the outcry over fiscal exploitation was loudest when the specific issues were jobs, salaries, and pensions. Time and time again Ceylonese would rise in the island's legislature to denounce the colonial government for paying British civil servants salaries and pensions far higher than the incomes received by most educated Ceylonese, and also for not replacing the British with educated Ceylonese, for whom, then as now, a civil service career tended to be the ultimate good.[7]

[4] Critical comments are found in legislative debates including *Legislative Council, 1926*, pp. 845, 1467; *State Council, 1931*, pp. 507, 1429; *1932*, pp. 1187, 2498; *1936*, pp. 1316, 1491, 2984; *1937*, pp. 2364-2420; *1941*, p. 211; *House of Representatives, 1948-49*, vol. 3, col. 1619-20; vol. 4, col. 1325-27; *1950-51*, vol. 8, col. 725-26. Also see *Report of the Kandyan Peasantry Commission*, pp. 12, 19, 202.

(Hereinafter the following abbreviations appear: debates in the Legislative Council—*Leg.*, debates in the State Council—*State*, debates in the House of Representatives—*House*, debates in the Senate—*Senate*, Volume—v., column—c.)

[5] See *Leg., 1925*, p. 327; *1926*, p. 912; *State, 1932*, p. 720; *1937*, pp. 1263-64; *House, 1952-53*, v. 12, c. 1083.

[6] This was one of the principal arguments for an income tax, finally enacted in 1932 with the backing of British officials. See *Leg., 1927*, p. 1018; *1928*, p. 2127; *1929*, p. 925; *1930*, pp. 770-920; *State, 1931*, pp. 444-55, 546-49, 1136, 1342-1435; *1932*, pp. 100-137.

[7] See *Leg., 1921*, pp. 176-99, 351; *1922*, pp. 421, 433, 581; *1923*, pp. 304-16, 343-44; *1924*, pp. 201-202; *1925*, pp. 325-26, 335-37, 495-96; *1926*, pp. 1109-84; *State, 1932*, pp. 2476, 3257-58.

Fiscal exploitation likewise became an issue during World War II, when London used its control over Ceylonese currency to inflate the local money supply and pay for goods and services with blocked sterling. A large part of the island's inhabitants appeared to rejoice in a wartime prosperity, but some critics pointed out that Britain's policy forced millions of low-income farmers and workers further to reduce their real level of consumption. This argument, stressed by the Left and occasionally employed by Ceylon's postwar Cabinets, was tied to the claim that Britain did not live up to its obligations to furnish Ceylon with adequate wartime supplies, and was used to press London for a more rapid thaw of frozen assets.[8]

But British wartime controls over the island's economy did not arouse nearly as much indignation as the textile quota imposed in 1934, three years after Britain had given Ceylon semiautonomy.[9] During negotiations over imperial tariff preferences the State Council had agreed to discriminate against various imports from outside the Empire, but it had refused to discriminate against Japanese textiles, since their low prices made them very attractive to the island's consumers. London doubly antagonized the nationalists when it made use of its reserve power to impose the quota. Politically, the action looked like a retrograde step, and economically, it looked like a wealthy country's decision to thrust part of the burden of its own unemployment upon desperately poor Ceylon. Nationalists brushed aside the British argument that Japanese "unfair competition" made the quotas essential.

About a decade earlier, leading Ceylonese spokesmen had attacked the British rubber restriction program as exploitative, arguing that it injured Ceylon to aid British interests in Malaya. But opinion on that question was divided.[10]

Ceylonese complaints described above relate to the colonial government's actions and include the charge that that government unduly favored British capitalists. The nationalists, however, have not regarded British capitalists solely as passive recipients of government favors. Instead they have looked on them as active exploiters in

[8] See *State*, *1942*, p. 1603; *1943*, pp. 45-54; *House*, *1947-48*, v. 1, c. 411-16, 859-1230.
[9] See *State*, *1934*, pp. 1393-1473; *1935*, pp. 12-13, 147, 299-318, 2129, 2273, 4156; *1936*, p. 937.
[10] See *Leg.*, *1922*, pp. 682-99; *1924*, pp. 242-57.

their own right. Among the more frequent accusations have been monopoly, unfair competition, discrimination against the Ceylonese, and the employment of aliens.[11] Many critics continue to bring these charges today, although political independence and Ceylonese advances in the business world have tended to make the accusations less sweeping.

Monopoly, as Ceylonese have used the term, has often had a very loose meaning. Much of the time it appears to have meant little more than that all the firms in the trade were British; nationality of ownership, rather than extent of competition, was the criterion. At other times the term has denoted a combination or monopolistic agreement, but much talk of British "combines" seems to have been based on the implicit assumption that foreign capitalists almost invariably get together to freeze out newcomers and exploit consumers. Nationalists of the Left have expressed the same attitude by their frequent references to "monopoly capitalism."

The complaint that the British have, in this looser sense, been monopolists has been closely connected with the complaints that they compete unfairly by using their financial strength to crush rivals and that they discriminate against the Ceylonese. Thus the accusers have often pictured British bankers denying loans to Ceylonese would-be businessmen in order to keep the island's trade a monopolistic preserve for British merchants. Similarly, the picture shows bankers and merchants refusing to train Ceylonese as managers, because of the fear that such training would endanger their monopolies.

The hiring of British executives is, of course, one part of the charge that British capitalists exploit Ceylon by employing aliens. But, as the earlier reference to Indian plantation workers has indicated, nationalist dislike of foreign firms' hiring practices covers the employment of wage labor as well. Indeed, many Ceylonese politicians and publicists have placed much more emphasis on Indian labor than on British management, believing it to be the greater threat because of

[11] Among numerous references are those in *Leg.*, *1921*, pp. 796-97; *1923*, pp. 628-33; *1926*, pp. 845-46; *1927*, p. 1010; *State*, *1932*, p. 1135; *1935*, pp. 670, 680-83, 714, 730; *1937*, pp. 78-84, 606-74; *1938*, pp. 465-66, 478-82, 3972; *1939*, pp. 4522-23; House, *1947-48*, v. 1, c. 118-21, 983, 1090; v. 2, c. 2790; *1948-49*, v. 3, c. 1046; v. 4, c. 1475; v. 5, c. 1574; *1949-50*, v. 7, c. 735; *1950-51*, v. 8, c. 1135, 2408; *1952-53*, v. 12, c. 915. Also see *Report of the Ceylon Banking Commission* (Sessional Paper XXII, 1934), pp. 22-28; *University of Ceylon Review*, X (April, 1952), 183-84; *Ceylon Journal of Industry and Commerce*, Feb., 1954, p. 3.

the greater numbers involved.[12]   When a Sinhalese objects to the presence of Indians, he is likely to have in mind some threat to his culture and national existence as well as to the racial distribution of jobs and income.[13]

Some Ceylonese nationalists have, with the aid of Marxist theory, combined all the charges of exploitation into an attack on British "colonial capitalism," seen as a planned and exploitative system. According to this view Britain acquired Ceylon as a colony in order to have a source of cheap raw materials, a ready market for manufactures, and an area for profitable investment.   In pursuit of their joint goal, the thesis continues, the colonial government and the capitalists assiduously encouraged and supported plantation agriculture and related foreign trade, but discouraged and put obstacles in the way of Ceylonese enterprise and "truly national" economic development.

Nationalists expounding this thesis have seen in the island's economic pattern the essence of exploitation and subservience.[14]   Even when not adhering to the Marxist theory of value, which pictures all profit as robbery, they have deemed it obvious that a system which pays its highest rewards to foreign (often absentee) capitalists is crudely exploitative.   Moreover, they have looked upon an economy which relies heavily on agricultural exports and manufactured imports as one that results in a manifestly weak trading position, one which no country would long endure if foreign rule did not prevent escape. Some Ceylonese have also accused the British of deliberately weaken-

---

[12] At times, however, a Ceylonese majority in the State Council favored active recruitment of additional Indian labor for the plantations.   Among the debates were those recorded in *Leg.*, *1925*, pp. 329-30; *1928*, p. 1729; *State*, *1934*, pp. 558-66, 3141-85; *1936*, pp. 393-95, 1315-16, 1433, 1491-92, 2984-92; *1937*, pp. 2364-2420; *1943*, pp. 1395-98; *1947*, pp. 795-802; *House*, *1947-48*, v. 1, c. 211, 654; *1954-55*, v. 18, c. 714.

[13] Sinhalese-speaking descendants of the island's ancient inhabitants form about 70 per cent of Ceylon's total population and about 85 per cent of its citizens. They are predominantly Buddhist.   Most non-Sinhalese on the island speak Tamil and are predominantly Hindu, with a large Muslim minority.   Indian Tamils now outnumber the Sinhalese in the highland plantation areas.

[14] Views of this general type can be found in *Leg.*, *1925*, pp. 326-27; *1926*, pp. 845-48; *1929*, pp. 1455-57; *State*, *1943*, pp. 1444-48; *House*, *1947-48*, v. 1, c. 386, 920-21, 962, 1289; *1950-51*, v. 8, c. 334; *1954-55*, v. 17, c. 1041-42; *Ceylon Economist*, April, 1919, pp. 66-67; November, 1919, p. 225; *Young Ceylon*, Sept., 1941, p. 103; Lanka Putra, *Mother Lanka*, pp. 9, 27-31, 38; D. C. Vijayavardhana, *Revolt in the Temple*, p. 466.

ing Ceylon by ruining its peasantry and making the country dependent upon foreign markets and supplies.

Finally, the Ceylonese holding these views were aware that the colonial government had in various ways encouraged plantation agriculture, and they looked upon the absence of vigorous promotional policies for other sectors as proof that Britain was determined to keep Ceylon in an inferior economic position. They were especially enraged by the colonial government's investing its surplus funds outside the island instead of lending those funds to Ceylonese investors.[15] Like German and Japanese neo-mercantilists, Ceylonese nationalists thought that the government should be a major and ever-active instrument for promoting prosperity and progress—and that a Government of Ceylon should promote the prosperity and progress of Ceylonese.[16] Sins of omission as well as sins of commission ranked high among those ascribed to British colonial capitalism.

Rather similar sins of omission are today charged to "Western economic imperialism." In Leftist and certain other Ceylonese circles the West is viewed as an exploiter taking advantage of "underdeveloped" countries by not aiding them to "develop," as well as by selling at unfairly high and buying at unfairly low prices.[17] Moreover, in these circles foreign offers of aid are suspect, as probable attempts to control economic change to the West's advantage. One fairly common accusation is that the West tries to block industrial advance by tying governmental aid to agricultural programs. Another that appears to be more widely believed is that foreign private capital wishes to enter Ceylon in order to choke off local industrial growth. Such fears do not seem to vanish when the record shows that little foreign private capital wishes to enter.

Because of Britain's political withdrawal from south Asia and

[15] See *Leg.*, *1919*, p. 184; *1925*, p. 383; *1926*, pp. 845-48, 939, 1520-24, 1539-42; *1927*, p. 1010; *State*, *1931*, p. 389. There is a similar complaint about insurance companies' funds in *Ceylon Economic Journal*, III (Dec., 1931), 5.

[16] Especially see *Leg.*, *1925*, pp. 326-27; *1926*, pp. 845-46; *1930*, p. 1082. Also see numerous passages in the *Ceylon Economist* of 1919-20. (This periodical should not be confused with its namesake of the post-1950 period.)

[17] References include *House*, *1949-50*, v. 6, c. 15, 45-46, 413, 537, 809, 818, 1295-1300, 1337; v. 7, c. 171-76; *1950-51*, v. 8, c. 997-98, 1135, 2416; *1951-52*, v. 10, c. 114, 221-22, 996, 1021-22; *1952-53*, v. 12, c. 286-94, 1138-39, 1219-20, 1640, 3849; v. 13, c. 3040; *1953-54*, v. 14, c. 500; v. 15, c. 200, 1018, 1788; *1954-55*, v. 17, c. 471, 512-20, 699; v. 18, c. 390, 961-62, 1139, 1377. Also see *Ceylon Economist*, I (Feb., 1951), 289-93; II (Sept., 1951), 5-7, 54; IV (Sept., 1954), 6-8.

Britain's and America's changed positions in world affairs, much of the cry of exploitation has recently been directed against the United States.[18]   Washington's refusal to pay a higher price for rubber and its denying aid because of Ceylon's rubber shipments to China came under bitter attack from all political parties.   Before the Suez Crisis, general talk about "economic imperialism" mentioned the United States much more frequently than Ceylon's former master. But British "colonial capitalism" still came under attack, partly as an ally of the capitalist power across the Atlantic, partly as the personification of the many British-owned firms dominating the economic landscape in Ceylon.

Indian capitalists complete the roster of foreigners and foreign groupings widely accused of exploitation.[19]   Indian money-lenders, who usually advance small sums at high interest rates to needy borrowers, are about as popular as one might guess.   Indian merchants share in charges directed against other foreign firms, charges that they compete unfairly, form combines to freeze out rivals and rob consumers and suppliers, and tend to employ their own countrymen.   Indian laborers are bitterly disliked as men who rob Ceylonese of jobs and represent a threat to Sinhalese culture, but it would not be correct to say that nationalists accuse them of exploitation.   The employer's offer, rather than the Indian worker's acceptance of a job, bears the onus.[20]

National Economic Independence

"Foreign exploitation" has been primarily a theme of complaint; its essence is foreign wickedness and Ceylonese injury.   When nationalists have announced a goal of action, they have more frequently talked about "national economic independence"; the essence of this concept is Ceylonese power.[21]   The two concepts are of course

[18] See, *inter alia, House, 1949-50,* v. 6, c. 413, 537, 555, 809, 814; v. 7, c. 171-76; *1950-51,* v. 8, c. 2940-63; *1951-52,* v. 10, c. 217, 268, 996; *1952-53,* v. 12, c. 286,1640; *1953-54,* v. 15, c. 200, 1018; *1954-55,* v. 17, c. 471, 520; *Ceylon Economist,* I (Nov., 1950), 107-14; (Feb., 1951), 215-18.

[19] Among references are *State, 1932,* p. 3256; *1936,* pp. 1315-16, 1421-23; *House, 1948-49,* v. 5, c. 1679-80; *1949-50,* v. 6, c. 703; *1954-55,* v. 18, c. 714; *Public Opinion,* March, 1942, pp. 11-12; *Young Ceylon,* Aug., 1942, p. 67.

[20] See above, this chapter, nn. 4, 12, 13.

[21] Another common nationalist phrase is "transition from colonial to national economy." .This is roughly synonymous with "achievement of national economic independence."   References to the economic-independence concept include *State, 1934,* p. 1396; *1935,* p. 2465; *1936,* p. 1369; *1945,* c. 930-31; *House, 1947-48,*

closely related, since the presence of the one suggests the absence of the other. Nationalists argue that, as long as the island suffers from the oppression of foreign exploiters, the Ceylonese people are not truly free, and that, when Ceylon does achieve economic independence, it will no longer allow itself to be exploited. The exact relationship between exploitation and independence is not always clear, but the goal of national economic freedom obviously has a dual aspect, involving both economic advantage and independence as a good in itself.

INDEPENDENCE WITHIN CEYLON

Much of the cry for economic independence relates to decision-making within the island's boundaries. When Ceylon gained dominion status, foreigners ceased to make legislative and other governmental decisions. They continued, however, to make a high percentage of business decisions, as managers, directors, and shareholders of plantation, commercial, manufacturing, and financial enterprises. Foreigners also continued to derive incomes from salaries, profits, and dividends, and nationalists did not overlook this fact when they demanded Ceylonization of employment and ownership. Legislators have been quite frank in saying that local jobs and resources should provide incomes for local people, and have pointed to laws and realities elsewhere to defend their position. But nationalists also regard foreign decision-making within Ceylon as an evil in itself, an evil which must at times be suffered because of the costs of a remedy, but which must always be disliked.

Nor, even if he is an economist, is a Ceylonese nationalist likely to pay much attention to the subtle argument that, since all business enterprise is subject to the market, no business executive can be a decision-maker in other than a superficial sense or in the short run. The average nationalist is not familiar with the theory of atomistic competition, and the economist is aware that few foreign-owned firms in Ceylon behave as atomistic competitors except when they sell to or buy from foreign markets.

Among the possible ways of transferring ownership and economic

---

v. 1, c. 43, 886, 1022; *1948-49*, v. 3, c. 1496; *1949-50*, v. 7 c. 897, 1973; *1950-51*, v. 8, c. 659-61, 1331; *1951-52*, v. 10, c. 470; 1952-53, v. 12, c. 290; Report of the *Ceylon Banking Commission*, Dec., 1934, p. 9; *Young Writer*, Sept. 30, 1941, p. 2; D. C. Vijayavardhana, *Revolt in the Temple*, pp. 109, 633.

power within the country are nationalizing, regulating, and taxing foreign properties, the private purchase of such properties, and the entry and growth of local rivals. Ceylonese nationalists have at various times proposed all these paths to Ceylonization. The more socialistically inclined have preferred that the island's government, rather than Ceylonese capitalists, play the leading role within the economy. Friends of private enterprise have advocated programs involving comparatively little state ownership and control. To date the policies actually adopted have been fairly mild and have altered the significance more than the appearance of foreign economic power.

There has not been any large-scale nationalization program. The Communist and semi-Trotskyist parties that represent the far Left in Ceylon have long asked for confiscation, without compensation, of foreign-owned land and business establishments—along with similar treatment of local capitalists, whom they condemn as "collaborators," a "comprador class" and the like.[22] But the Marxist parties have never won a large part of the total vote. The People's United Front, which captured the 1956 Parliament through a coalition of Sinhalese communalists[23] and various Leftist elements, drew up an election platform which read: "All key industries must be run by the State. . . . All essential industries, including foreign-owned plantations, transport, banking and insurance will be progressively nationalized." But postelection pronouncements have been vague as to when and how the nationalization will take place.[24] The prime minister has consistently stated that Ceylon will pay fair compensation.

Plausible reasons why Ceylon's government has not nationalized foreign properties are easy to discover. The island's record of government enterprise has not been happy; foreign and local investigating committees alike have condemned it for general inefficiency

[22] See *House, 1947-48*, v. 1, c. 1194; *1948-49*, v. 3, c. 857, 1229-30; v. 5, c. 453-54; *1949-50*, v. 7, c. 727, 838; *1953-54*, v. 14, c. 1162; *1955-56*, v. 21, c. 1020.

[23] In Ceylon linguistic and religious groups are called "communities." "Communalism" is a sort of "community" nationalism.

[24] See *Free Lanka*, March 11, 1956; *Ceylon News*, May 3, 1956, p. 9; May 24, 1956, p. 7; Oct. 25, 1956, p. 20.

and a host of particular mistakes.[25]   The United National party, headed by essentially conservative politicians, had no desire to multiply onerous responsibilities and simultaneously establish a precedent distasteful to Ceylon's own capitalists.   Finally, the Cabinet feared that it could not quickly pay British owners full compensation, and realized that a British boycott could ruin the Ceylonese economy. This last thought may well cause even the People's United Front indefinitely to postpone its promised nationalization.

But, while no seizure of foreign properties has occurred, government action has brought about substantial transfer of income and economic power.   In part it has achieved this by directly substituting governmental for private decision, via both market controls and the collection of taxes.   Just as foreign capitalists' predominance gives Leftism in Ceylon a strongly nationalist tinge, so there is a nationalist aspect to state intervention, which enables Ceylonese legislators and bureaucrats to prescribe limits to permitted business behavior.   Similarly, higher income taxes have brought about a substantial redistribution of economic power, since foreign capitalists thereby have less to spend and a Ceylonese Parliament governs the uses of the funds.

The closest approach to nationalization of foreign properties has been the government's reserving certain resources and industries as the exclusive domain of the state.   Thus for about a decade the government has been a monopolistic importer of rice, shutting out Indian and other merchants who would otherwise transact this business.   State-sponsored co-operative stores have sold the rice, thereby diminishing Indian trade at the retail level.[26]   Ceylon's well advertised sale of rubber to Communist China has also diverted trade from foreign firms, in this case, from British exporters.[27]

During the late 1940's and early 1950's the government's announced policy was not to let any private firm enter "basic" manufacturing industries; in this way it may have kept out a few

---

[25] See International Bank for Reconstruction and Development Mission, *The Economic Development of Ceylon* (Baltimore: The John Hopkins Press, 1953), chap. xv; *Report of the Commission on Government Commercial Undertakings* (Ceylon Government Press, Nov., 1953), chap. iii; *Ceylon Daily News*, Aug. 19, 1955 (summary of Japanese mission's report in "Economic Supplement").

[26] See *House, 1947-48*, v. 1, c. 2149-50; *1954-55*, v. 19, c. 1221.

[27] See *House, 1954-55*, v. 19, c. 62.

foreign firms expressing interest in Ceylon.[28]   After 1953 government policy changed; Ceylon actively, if cautiously, invited foreign private capital to enter various lines of manufacturing; but the United National party's defeat came before the changed policy had produced substantial results.   The 1956 election apparently has meant a return to the old policy of reserving new "key" industries for the state,[29] although the Cabinet has been vague concerning times and methods of actual nationalization.

Ceylon's government has also reserved certain areas of business for local private enterprise.   One method has been the use of import and export quotas; thus, only Ceylonese firms receive quotas for "new" trade, such as that resumed with Germany and Japan.[30] Another method has been restriction of foreign entry. Vocal Leftism and nationalism have done much of the job without government help, frightening away foreign capital that otherwise might wish to enter, but legal restriction has reduced the inflow even further.   Land policy has for about two decades denied foreigners the right to buy public land.

Finally, government restrictive action has transferred income and economic power by forcing foreign firms to hire more Ceylonese. To date the rules that govern hiring have not made leading foreign businesses replace their top men with citizens, but a schedule has been set for increasing the percentage of Ceylonese managers and lieutenants.   This will reduce the number of salaried Indians as well as salaried Europeans, and will in effect shut down some Indian businesses that depend on family management.   Cabinets have in recent years sought also to Ceylonize wage employment by repatriating Indian laborers, but were largely blocked in this attempt by New Delhi's insistence that few of the workers were

[28] "Basic" was defined very broadly. "From the economic point of view an industry may serve a basic need of the community or it may be of such a character as to tend to become a monopoly, the exercise of which owing to circumstances can be detrimental to the interests of the community. Socially, an industry may supply a commodity which is essential to public health, or the condition or the quality of which closely affects public health" *(Report on Industrial Development and Policy* [Sessional Paper XV, 1946], p. 16).

[29] See *Ceylon News,* July 19, 1956, p. 16; Sept. 13, 1956, p. 16.

[30] The Cabinet elected in April, 1956, has substantially increased the lines of trade reserved for Ceylonese exporters. See *Ceylon News,* July 12, 1956, p. 18; Sept. 13, 1956, p. 16.

Indian nationals. The People's United Front has promised that it will act more vigorously to vacate jobs for the island's citizens.

Other governmental methods of building up Ceylonese commerce and industry, and thus of shifting the balance of economic power between local and foreign interests, have been easier credit and aid through research. Such measures have been part of official policy since the 1930's. When the International Bank Mission made its report in 1952, however, the credit institutions, research agencies, and other bodies set up to aid Ceylonese private business had accomplished little.[31] Such growth as had occurred was largely attributable to private finance and entrepreneurship. Additional agencies were established during 1954-56 and appear initially to have been somewhat more successful, but their history is of course very short.[32]

Ceylonese financial policy has helped local capitalists buy plantations from the British. Government-sponsored credit agencies have helped to provide purchasers with funds, and exchange control has not prevented the British sellers from converting rupees into pounds. Large-scale transfers of plantation properties have occurred in this way. But nationalists of the Left and other government critics have by no means been pleased, since they would have preferred that Ceylon use its pound holdings to add to physical capital on the island. Although the transfers Ceylonized ownership, the critics reasoned, the capital outflow harmed the cause of true economic independence.[33]

This points towards a second major aspect of national economic freedom.

INDEPENDENCE IN THE WORLD ECONOMY

Much of the demand for national economic independence concerns relationships between Ceylon and the rest of the world. Nationalists have seen both economic disadvantage and political humiliation in Ceylon's heavy reliance upon export of agricultural raw materials and import of manufactured goods and food, and in

[31] See International Bank Mission, *The Economic Development of Ceylon*, pp. 517-18, 797.
[32] See below, chap. iv, pp. 85-87.
[33] See *House*, *1952-53*, v. 12, c. 1664; *1953-54*, v. 14, c. 1837; *1954-55*, v. 18, c. 1042-43.

the chiefly agricultural character of the economy. A more diversified pattern of production, involving a greater degree of self-sufficiency, is their prescription.

In so far as the arguments for diversification relate to economic advantage, they do not necessarily involve nationalist sentiment. Foreign advisers as well as Ceylonese have suggested that the island strive to be less dependent upon tea, rubber, and coconuts and that it increase local production of rice and other essential goods.[34] The history of the last thirty years shows just how vulnerable Ceylon's economy is to wars and recessions. After 1929, and again after the Korean War, the terms of international trade turned sharply against agricultural-export nations. During World War II Japan's conquest of Burma and Germany's destruction of British merchant ships threatened a disastrous shortage of food. Moreover, some diversification appears essential for any substantial long-run increase in per capita income; densely populated Ceylon cannot raise living standards very much through agriculture alone.

But even when the argument is purely economic, nationalist emotion often shines through the language. The positive theme that Ceylon shall become secure and prosperous is closely joined with the negative theme that imperialists and colonialists shall not keep this from happening. Ceylonese often blame the countries with which they trade for unfavorable changes in price ratios; they have especially denounced the United States for not paying higher prices for natural rubber.[35]

Political and quasi-political advantages claimed for economic diversification have been varied and frequently vague. One argument is that Ceylon's economy now makes it vulnerable to powerful nations that may try to take political advantage of their positions as importers and exporters. This reasoning, of course, leads to a desire not only for greater self-sufficiency, but also for greater diversification of trade. Ceylonese nationalists of both Left and Right have favored seeking alternative markets and thus decreasing dependence upon the English-speaking peoples.[36]

Another argument is that greater self-sufficiency means greater

---

[34] See International Bank Mission, *op. cit.*, pp. 16-19, 23, 40.
[35] See above, this chapter, n. 17.
[36] See, *inter alia*, House, *1952-53*, v. 13, c. 1224-25; *1954-55*, v. 18, c. 1139.

freedom in economic planning, and that the ability to plan is a highly desirable form of independence. This line of thought comes chiefly from the Left and tends to merge with emphasis on a special pattern of diversification, the development of heavy industry.

Some nationalists appear to regard self-sufficiency as a good in itself, to believe that a country should, whenever possible, eliminate foreign influences. A few have gone so far as to glorify the island's ancient autarchic economy, when feudal agriculture reigned supreme. To press home their argument that Ceylon could easily feed its population, some orators have pictured the ancient kingdom with two to three times the present number of people, all enjoying agricultural abundance.[37] That variety of nationalism which emphasizes the culture of traditional Ceylon has in general also emphasized peasant farming; its imagination has been captured by the reconquest of jungle land that once supported the splendors of Ceylon's ancient capitals; in extreme form it has demanded that British plantations become parts of village farming areas.

It would be absurdly incorrect, however, to picture the demand for greater self-sufficiency as a cry for twentieth-century agricultural autarchy. Nationalist emphasis upon Ceylonese manufacturing has also been strong; the charge that the colonial regime prevented industrial growth was one of the main accusations brought against the British. Greater self-sufficiency has meant—and to many has especially meant—the growth of local manufactures as well as the increased production of food. Dudley Senanayake summarized widespread opinion when he declared, " . . . the progress of a country, its place in the civilized world, is judged by the extent of industrialization achieved."[38] Witness also the "planning" argument mentioned above.

A related point is that, although Ceylonese nationalists have thought that their own country's dependence on foreign trade shows a lack of freedom, they have not drawn the same conclusions concerning all other countries. Thus, although Great Britain relies

[37] See, for instance, S. W. Dassenaike's remarks in *State, 1932,* p. 2462. Chap. ii of N. K. Sarkar, "Demography of Ceylon in the Twentieth Century" (unpublished doctoral thesis, University of London, 1954) considers various estimates of ancient Ceylon's population and puts the maximum possible figure at seven million, or about the 1946 population.

[38] *State, 1944,* p. 437. In 1947 Senanayake entered, and during 1952-53 he headed, a Cabinet that stressed agricultural expansion.

heavily on overseas markets and sources of supply, they have not thought that this makes the British economy subservient. Rather, they have looked on export of manufactures and import of materials as a symbol of dominance, or even of "economic imperialism." Not dependence on foreign trade, but on raw-material exports and manufactured imports, has to them seemed the essence of economic bondage.

Price analysis and economic history offer some justification for this distinction. Before the days of state trading agencies and state regulation of output and prices, agricultural commodities and other raw materials entering into foreign trade were more generally sold under highly competitive conditions than were manufactured goods. Moreover, Ceylon's leading exports have chiefly gone to a very few countries, whereas Britain's trade was widely scattered. But the principal reason for the nationalists' exaltation of manufacturing and poor opinion of agriculture appears to be much simpler. The manufacturing countries have been, fairly generally, those possessing overseas colonies and/or major military power; the exceptions to this rule have not impressed themselves on the minds of Ceylonese nationalists. On the other hand, most of the overseas colonies have had few factories and have depended heavily on agricultural or other raw-material exports. The economic patterns accompanying major-power and colonial status became, for colonial peoples, symbols of dominance and dependence.[39]

Some government action to make Ceylon less dependent on plantation crops commenced as early as 1916, when the colonial governor appointed an Industries Commission to study the island's resources and recommend concerning their development. But little even was planned until the 1930's,[40] when the semi-autonomous State Council set up a Department of Commerce and Industries and commenced a series of irrigation projects to expand the food-growing area. Wartime shortages intensified effort to swell both agricultural and manufacturing output, and the government's announced policy in postwar years has been to push development along both lines. It has, however, put major emphasis on food production.

In its attempts to make Ceylon more nearly self-sufficient in food

[39] Some Ceylonese nationalists argue that South American countries' economic patterns show that they are political dependencies.

[40] Work on a hydroelectric system began in 1924, but no power was produced until after World War II.

the government has employed various trade barriers, including import duties, import quotas, and an Agricultural Products Act compelling traders to buy a certain percentage of their supplies from local sources. But these have applied primarily to other foodstuffs than the major import, rice. On the whole, government policy has put much greater emphasis on devices other than those usually called to mind by the term "economic nationalism." The goal of greater self-sufficiency, rather than the particular methods employed, has been the principal reflection of nationalist sentiment.

Chief among the methods have been the "colonization" projects, whereby the government clears, irrigates, and improves land in the Dry Zone, thus creating homesteads which it releases to peasants and "middle class" farmers. Closely akin to this is the village expansion program, which makes lands surrounding the villages available and suitable for the neighborhood's peasants. The government has also sought to increase yield per acre by training farmers in more efficient methods, especially in the Japanese method of transplanting paddy. To provide the necessary finances it has advanced loans through co-operative societies, and to provide incentive it has guaranteed a minimum purchase price for rice and other foods.

To characterize the food-production program as solely a drive for greater self-sufficiency would be unjust. In perhaps a more important sense it is an attempt to raise income by putting unemployed farm labor on unutilized land and by increasing yields. The background of the program consists of landlessness and farm poverty as well as huge imports of rice. But speeches and other pronouncements make it quite clear that one major purpose of the agricultural program has been to make Ceylon less dependent on foreign food.

In its more modest industrial development program the government has, in varying degrees, combined protectionism, state aid, and state enterprise. As in the case of agriculture, protectionist devices have included import duties, import quotas, and a statute, the Industrial Products Act, compelling traders to buy certain percentages of their supplies from local producers.[41] These trade barriers have played a more significant role in the encouragement of

[41] For a description of these barriers, see International Bank Mission, *op. cit.*, pp. 145-51, and *Report of the Taxation Commission* (Sessional Paper XVII, 1955), chap. xxv.

manufacturing than in the food-production drive; without them, few new enterprises would have entered the field against foreign suppliers. Industrialists and other nationalist critics, however, have denounced the government for not keeping out imports to a still greater extent.[42] The prewar State Council gave protection to only a few minor industries, such as soap and matches; postwar barriers have not stimulated widespread growth.[43]

Among the issues involved in the controversy are the technical serviceability of local manufactures and their conformity to Western criteria of excellence. Some nationalists denounce the island's high-income consumers as snobbish and Western in their tastes, and charge that a similar snobbery and Westernism have accounted for legislators' and administrators' reluctance to make trade barriers more exclusive. Closely allied to this is the plea that Ceylonese consumers should, like Indians, take a patriotic interest in their country's manufactures and insist on buying "Swadeshi." Protectionists are especially angered by the scornful attitude frequently displayed towards local goods.[44]

State aid to private manufacturing enterprise began in the 1930's, with the establishment of an industrial research bureau, the training of technicians, governmental granting of small loans, and sponsorship of the Bank of Ceylon. These steps did not result in much growth of private industry, however, and during the Second World War the State Council began to emphasize state enterprise instead. A 1946 policy statement reserved "basic" industries for the government and left the remainder of the manufacturing field to government, private, and "mixed" enterprise all three.[45]

This continued to be the official policy until the 1952-53 debate over the International Bank Mission's report. But state enterprise

[42] See *Ceylon Journal of Industry and Commerce*, Nov., 1952, p. 3; July, 1953, p. 1; Aug., 1953, pp. 5-7; *Ceylon Observer*, Sept. 6, 1955; Sept. 27, 1955; Oct. 11-12, 1955; Nov. 19, 1955.

[43] The 1952 *Census of Industry* listed 692 industrial establishments (inclusive of coconut oil mills, but exclusive of tea factories and rubber mills) employing 53,-457 persons. Engineering, coconut and oil milling, coir, and printing, book-binding, and kindred industries accounted for two-thirds of the employment. In 1955 the Planning Secretariat reported, "The fundamental characteristics of the economy remain much the same as they were described in *1922* . . . Industrialization has made very little headway" (*Six-year Programme of Investment*, p. 236; my italics).

[44] See *Ceylon Observer*, Sept. 6, 1955; Nov. 19, 1955.

[45] *Report on Industrial Development and Policy*, pp. 15-23.

did not have a favorable record, and earlier plans for new government factories seem to have come under question before the Mission's report led to a new statement of policy.[46] During 1954-56 the government placed emphasis on privately owned factories and "industrial partnership" between the state and private capital. Among the statutes of this period were those setting up an Institute of Scientific and Industrial Research and creating a Development Finance Corporation with the power to buy shares and advance loans.

The pre-1956 regime also actively, if cautiously, invited foreign private enterprise to help develop Ceylonese industry, and borrowed from the International Bank in order to help finance its general development program. In spite of the facts that it did not join SEATO and sold rubber to Communist China, its opponents charged it with attempts to sell Ceylon to capitalist, imperialist America. The new Cabinet, heading a semisocialist, fervently nationalist coalition, talks once more of stressing government enterprise and is not likely either to seek or to attract much foreign private capital.

To the extent that foreign private enterprise is required to make Ceylon more nearly self-sufficient in manufactures, there is obviously a clash between national economic independence, defined as increased Ceylonization of economic power on the island, and national economic independence, defined as decreased reliance on export and import markets. The emotional appeal of the former goal is perhaps the greater, and tied to it is the self-interest of those Ceylonese who hope to develop local industries. It is not likely that any government will offer foreign investors terms that will cause a large volume of private capital to flow into Ceylon, partly because favorable terms would be politically risky, partly because foreign investors fear that a later government will be less friendly.

[46] See *Report of the Commission on Government Commercial Undertakings*, pp. 5-6.

Note on Communalism, Economics, and Language

Ceylon is a multicommunal nation. The Sinhalese, Ceylon Tamil, Moor, Malay, and Burgher "communities" that together constitute the Ceylonese people as defined by Ceylonese law are keenly aware of differences among themselves as well as of their separateness from the foreign world. Moreover, within the majority Sinhalese community a sense of unity is accompanied by acute awareness of significant distinctions—Buddhist majority and Christian minority, Sinhalese-educated majority and English-educated minority, lowlanders (more Westernized) and Kandyans (less Westernized). English education and the Christian religion also reduce, to a much smaller extent, the sense of unity among the Tamils.

The nationalism discussed in Chapter 2 was that of Ceylonese against "foreign" peoples, including the hundreds of thousands of Indian Tamils long resident on the island who insist that they too are Ceylonese. But nationalist emotions are not separate from communalist emotions. Especially among the majority Sinhalese is the determination that Ceylon shall be truly independent associated with the resolve that their own community shall come into its own. Past history and present fears make this almost inevitable. Ancient Ceylon was a Sinhalese nation, and before the coming of the Europeans the traditional invader was the Tamil from south India; more recently the British plantations were carved out of Sinhalese districts, and the Indian migrants who came to work on them were Tamils from the traditional enemy area.

Communalist sentiment as well as nationalist sentiment has economic significance, since communalists, like nationalists, make a distinction between "us" and "them" and regard as unjust any distribution of income, wealth, opportunity, and power which gives "outsiders" too great a share of the spoils.[1] When, during the struggle for Ceylon's independence, Tamil leaders asked that their minority community receive half of the legislative seats, they seem to have been motivated in part by a fear that Tamils would not otherwise be

---

[1] See G. C. Mendis, "The Causes of Communal Conflict in Ceylon," *University of Ceylon Review*, I (April, 1943), 41-49.

able to retain their high percentage of government jobs. In recent years a communal sense of grievance has been strongest among the majority Sinhalese, who as a whole are much less than proportionately represented at the university, in the better government jobs, and in the professions, partly—perhaps chiefly—because a smaller percentage of Sinhalese than Tamils were educated in English-speaking schools.[2] Among the Sinhalese the sense of injustice seems to be greatest among these with little or no knowledge of English, although the leaders of the discontented have come from the ranks of the English-educated.

This sense of economic grievance is one cause of the widespread demand that Sinhalese become the language of the central university, the central government, and the courts and government offices throughout the Sinhalese areas of the island. Such a step, its advocates have argued, would establish greater equality of opportunity—or, at least, greater equality among the majority community. With English no longer a requisite of university education, the better government jobs, and professional success, the Sinhalese-educated could compete on equal terms with those who know English well. To the criticism that most Tamils and Burghers do not know Sinhalese, hence could not enjoy equal opportunity, the advocates of "Sinhalese only!" reply that it is not feasible for the island to have two or three official languages, and majority rule must prevail. There is talk of establishing two new universities, one for Tamil- and one for English-speakers after the existing university has changed from English to Sinhalese, but the Sinhalese leaders are adamant that the bulk of government employees shall speak Sinhalese. Since civil service jobs are desperately sought prizes in Ceylon,[3] the potential economic significance of the changeover is great.

English- and Tamil-speakers also fear that, even if Ceylon's low income could be stretched to cover three universities, the new ones would be poor substitutes for the old, with inferior libraries and laboratories and less well-rounded staff. A more general criticism expressed by opponents of the shift from English is that the Sinhalese language is not now suitable for instruction in the natural and social

[2] See above, chap. 1 n. 22.
[3] Not only do such jobs offer social prestige and security, they are a high percentage of the well-paying jobs on the island.

sciences, that education in the secondary schools has already suffered, and that a further change from English to Sinhalese would prevent Ceylonese students from acquiring the necessary skills for administering and improving the nation's economy.[4]

During the 1956 election campaign the two largest parties, the United National party and the People's United Front, endorsed "Sinhalese only!" although there was considerable suspicion that only the latter intended to effect an over-all change from English in the near future. Shortly after the United Front's election victory, Parliament adopted Sinhalese as the island's official language and put pressure on the university to begin the transition from English. By the end of the year, however, only the Oriental Languages faculty announced themselves ready to make the change. Under rules adopted by the pre-1956 government, Ceylonese grammar and secondary schools had progressively increased the volume of instruction in Sinhalese and Tamil and reduced that in English. By 1956 most students were, in most subjects, taught in their parents' native tongue.

[4] For an expression of this viewpoint, see Sir Ivor Jennings (until 1955 Vice-Chancellor of the University of Ceylon), "Equality of Degradation," *Social Justice Annual*, 1952.

3

The Economic Role of the State

MOST CEYLONESE LEGISLATORS and publicists have assigned major economic roles to the state. In part this is attributable to nationalist ambitions; it has seemed unthinkable that the government do nothing to remedy this situation while foreign capital and management commanded the economic heights, Ceylonese incomes were far below Western levels, and national economic independence was only a dream. Nationalists have demanded that the state be promoter and protector, that it take on much of the burden of transferring income, wealth, and economic power from foreigners to citizens, changing Ceylon from a "colonial" to a "national" economy, and in other ways conferring upon the island the blessings of economic development.

Nationalist ambitions are not, however, the sole explanation of interventionism's strength in Ceylon. Especially during the past two decades much Ceylonese opinion has favored measures to bring about a somewhat more nearly equal distribution of income and opportunity and to help the sick, the unemployed, and the miserably poor. Moreover, the drive for economic development has had other as well as nationalist origins. Social conscience and group self-interest also led to demands for government action to transform the economy.

Apart from special nationalist features, most of the argument for intervention has taken familiar European forms. Because of their British tutelage, Ceylonese intellectuals have adopted or altered economic philosophies expounded at Oxford, Cambridge, and London; Ceylonese trends of thought have paralleled, although they have not exactly reproduced, trends in Britain. In general, economic opinion has become more interventionist and more egalitarian with the passing of the decades. During the interwar years a high percentage of university graduates emerged with views well to the Left of the modified liberals and conservative interventionists who were the legislators and spokesmen for the older generation. By the late 1930's the radical swing had become quite sharp, and in recent years most university students have been Left of the Gaitskell wing of British Labour; a high percentage have proclaimed themselves to be Trotskyists or Communists.

As in other countries, however, political trends have lagged behind intellectual currents. At least before 1956, the Leftward movement among Ceylon's legislators was much less pronounced than among its students and academicians. Nor does the 1956 election victory of the People's United Front seem to mark the end of the political lag. Although the winning coalition includes a party which until recently advertised itself as Trotskyist, and although the election platform promised large-scale nationalization, the coalition's principal strength appears to lie in the heightened nationalism of the Sinhalese-speaking majority. This nationalist sentiment does not now appear to require any particular economic ideology. Since Sinhalese traditions stem from an agrarian, feudal, caste-dominated Ceylon, they cannot provide a set of rules for contemporary economic policy, but they may strengthen attitudes hostile to Marxian Socialism as well as to other borrowings from Western culture.

The Interwar Period

CONSERVATIVE INTERVENTIONISM

During the nineteen-twenties and thirties most Ceylonese legislators and publicists were sufficiently interventionist, business-minded, and nonegalitarian to be described as neomercantilists. German and, especially, Japanese economic history excited their admiration and reinforced their belief that a "truly national" government could be a powerful engine of transformation and progress.[1] But, as in other countries, so in Ceylon: neomercantilism was not an integrated or a standardized body of doctrine so much as a shift-

---

[1] See *Leg.*, *1925*, p. 327; *1926*, pp. 845-46; *State*, *1932*, p. 2462; *Ceylon Economist*, April, 1919, p. 66; June, 1919, pp. 99-104; *Report of the Ceylon Banking Commission*, p. 69.

ing mixture of policies representing various degrees of reliance on individual initiative and state enterprise and control. Conservative interventionists shared the old-style liberals' belief that legal liberty is good, private property a bulwark to be protected, and hope of profit an indispensable incentive, although they were much readier than the liberals to assert that national goals take precedence over individual rights and that the government can confer greater over-all opportunity by curbing, directing, and aiding economic activities. They looked upon their policies as logical corollaries of nationalism, or as means of ending foreign exploitation and achieving national economic independence.

The opportunities in which the island's neomercantilists were chiefly interested were loans for Ceylonese borrowers, training for Ceylonese managers and subordinates, and improved competitive positions for Ceylonese firms.[2] Legislative debates and other state papers bring out leading characteristics of the dominant interventionist thought. A. Mahadeva's speech of July 23, 1926, provides perhaps the most spectacular example. In the course of his remarks, Mahadeva accused British merchants and bankers of monopolizing trade and investment opportunities on the island, argued that Ceylon could never progress on a purely agricultural basis, and urged that, if the colonial government were "not merely concerned with questions of good order and justice," it would take steps to aid Ceylonese enterprise and local industry and safeguard Ceylonese investors against competition from foreign capital. ". . . we want Government to give us a helping hand, foster our industries, lend us capital, prohibit more than a proportion of share capital being held outside the island, and so make us an industrially strong country."[3]

In 1934, three years after the State Council had taken over most legislative initiative from British officials, the *Report of the Ceylon Banking Commission* summarized in a more moderate manner much of the neomercantilists' economic philosophy: World War I

revealed the inherent weaknesses of the economic structure of a country whose material prosperity depended on the welfare of a few staple agricultural industries catering entirely for an export market. At the same time, a public, buoyed by the acquisition of a measure of political

[2] See the references in chap. 11, nn. 15, 16.
[3] *Leg., 1926*, pp. 845-46.

power, aspired to achieve a similar measure of freedom in the economic sphere. It was considered essential for the attainment of this goal of economic freedom that the public should have adequate financial assistance, so as to enable indigenous capital and enterprise to participate more actively in the trade and industries of the country, and, in particular, to cultivate and expand the home market in preference to the export markets. The prevailing banking system primarily designed to foster economic development by requisitioning the aid of non-indigenous capital and enterprise proved to be ill-adapted, by the very nature of its structure, to offer such facilities. The most urgent problem is the opening up of new industries, both agricultural and manufacturing, with the main object of catering primarily for the home market and thereby rendering the economy less susceptible to the vagaries of markets abroad.[4]

A year earlier, the Executive Committee of Labour, Industry and Commerce had spelled out their notions of proper government activities in the industrial field: "The functions of Government in relation to Industries may be said to be (a) to conduct necessary research work; (b) to erect model plants for the purposes of demonstration; (c) to finance private individuals for the purposes of demonstration and development."[5] There is reason to believe, however, that the Committee would also have recommended import restrictions, had they not realized that London still retained reserve powers that would enable them to veto such measures. For a while the State Council looked favorably upon protection of Ceylonese manufacturers via licensing and assigned output quotas, but after this method of protection resulted in poor quality of output in the match industry, a majority of legislators changed their minds. In 1940 they voted down a bill to extend the licensing system to other manufactures.[6]

Agricultural as well as industrial policies became more interventionist after Ceylonese lawmakers acquired legislative initiative. Except for controls on tea and rubber acreage and protective tariffs on certain minor foods, measures were not restrictionist, but the Council established greater self-sufficiency as a goal and regarded state pioneering, subsidization, and controls as necessary means. Con-

[4] *Report of the Ceylon Banking Commission*, pp. 9, 20.
[5] *State*, *1933*, p. 2234.
[6] See *State*, *1936*, pp. 1421-23; *1937*, pp. 78-79, 606-74; *1940*, pp. 194, 399-406.

trols related to the terms under which public lands were made available, and were nationalist in that they denied new areas to foreign capitalists, egalitarian in that they favored peasant proprietorship.[7]

Apart from the manufacturing, banking, and agricultural measures mentioned above, and the introduction of bargaining tariffs within the framework of an Imperial preference system, chief interventionist acts during the interwar period were the provision of work relief, the establishment of wage boards for plantation labor, and the regulation of certain other plantation conditions. These policies, like the encouragement of peasant agriculture, anticipated the more egalitarian interventionism of the wartime and postwar years. But the work relief was a response to truly massive unemployment supplemented by crop failures and a disastrous malaria epidemic, and the paternalism shown plantation labor came after pressure from New Delhi, which showed great interest in the wages and working conditions of Indian laborers on the island. Few Ceylon legislators as yet favored an extensive welfare state.

Among the unofficial publications which favored conservative interventionism, the *Ceylon Economist* of 1919-20 stood out because of its early, enthusiastic, and single-minded devotion to the cause of Ceylonese economic progress via promotional and protectionist policies.[8] From the first page of the first issue, which declared, "If the War has taught us any lesson, it is that we should never depend economically on any foreign country," editorials urged full speed on a development program inspired by Japan:

". . . what Japan has achieved by her diligence and research we can equally well acquire provided we are adventurous and progressive enough." "The general factors that contribute to the Industrial and Commercial progress of any country are [eight requirements]. . . . On all these heads the Government of Japan took the initiative, and all the initial losses and expenses incurred thereon were borne up by the Government." "The State must initiate all possible industrial

---

[7] See *Report of the Committee on Utilization of Crown Lands* (Sessional Paper III, 1953), pp. 7-11. The Land Development Ordinance of 1935 was based on the 1929 report of a Land Commission appointed in 1927.

[8] Published in Jaffna, the Tamil's leading city on the island, the *Ceylon Economist* at times showed a special interest in the development of the Tamil area of northern Ceylon.

ventures in these [recommended] areas with existing materials as well as indicate what new materials can be grown and how manipulated."[9]

Editors of the *Ceylon Economist* were very much in a hurry and very much afraid that foreign capital and management would dominate the economy: "We cannot afford to sit down and experiment with new things just at present. We shall be left behind. We are in need of capital to launch forth big commercial enterprises. It is only when we have the time and means that we can sit down and do research work." Ceylonese must not "allow the hordes of foreigners who will troop into this country, to do all the thinking for them in this matter of commercial, agricultural and industrial development."[10]

Legislator, writer, and lecturer, K. Balasingham was the most persistent advocate of tariff protection. A 1919 article in the *Ceylon Economist* urged customs duties to promote the local production of rice.[11] Most of his energies, however, were devoted to the cause of local manufactures. In 1931 he attempted to convert Liberal League critics to his protectionist cause: ". . . we can now use effectively the strong lever of protection to lift us out of the prevailing depression, and to provide work for the unemployed as England is doing today. . ." ". . . protection . . . is the usual weapon adopted by all nations to resist competition of foreign sweated labour, or to foster nascent industries."[12]

During the later 1930's perhaps the most interesting example of protectionist, interventionist thought was V. S. Sigurunathan's "What Is the Solution of the Youth of Ceylon to the Challenge of Our Time?," a brief article that won the first prize in *Young Ceylon's* 1938 essay competition.[13] Young Sigurunathan placed first emphasis upon agricultural expansion, but he believed that manufacturing also should be promoted and protected: "If our indigenous industries are developed on proper lines, they will usher in a new era of national prosperity." A "buy Ceylonese campaign" could ensure

[9] *Ceylon Economist*, April, 1919, p. 66; June, 1919, p. 100; Nov., 1919, p. 226.
[10] *Ibid.*, March, 1919, p. 26; April, 1919, pp. 66-67.
[11] *Ibid.*, March, 1919, p. 79.
[12] *Liberal Gazette*, Dec. 31, 1931, pp. 6-7.
[13] *Young Ceylon*, June, 1938, pp. 38-40.

"a brilliant economic future" for the island. High tariff walls should keep out foreign products. "Ceylon must be made more self-supporting."

Young Ceylon's prize essay differed from most earlier interventionist writings by calling for various welfare measures. The government, argued Sigurunathan, should protect children, provide poor relief, and extend medical aid, including prenatal and postnatal care for mothers. In this respect his article anticipated the more egalitarian interventionism of wartime and postwar years.

OLD-STYLE LIBERALISM

Because of nationalist ambitions, Gladstonian liberalism was not popular in Ceylon even during the 1920's. During most of the interwar period, however, Ceylonese modifications of old-style liberalism, which approved of much promotional but not of protectionist and egalitarian intervention, appealed to an appreciable minority among the English-educated, including a few of the island's legislators. Like their British counterparts, this minority stressed the sacredness of liberty and property and the immutable nature of the laws of supply and demand. Thus in 1934 W. A. de Silva cried that the "wretched system of protection . . . strikes at the root of liberty," and in 1926 he opposed regulation of plantation labor contracts, arguing that "the employee here is in a position of perfect freedom, and the employer has no power whatever to have any hold on his labour." In 1922 Sir Ponnambalam Ramanathan declared that the rubber restriction ordinance was "bound to be made futile by the laws of supply and demand"; and when in 1926 a British colonial official commented that "the days are gone by when laissez-faire is regarded as an automatic cure for all circumstances," E. W. Perera replied, "But still they [the laws of supply and demand] are true."[14]

The liberals' dislike of high public salaries and rising taxes was even greater. Time and again they raised the cry, "Retrench!" In 1919 Ramanathan tied his opposition to tax increases to a theory of justice, declaring, "Government transcends its powers . . . when it forcibly extracts this money from one set of pockets for the benefit of

[14] *Leg.*, *1922*, p. 690; *1926*, pp. 1466, 1687; *State*, *1934*, p. 1228.

another set of persons."[15]   In 1931 the short-lived Liberal League was formed to fight the income tax proposed in that year. The *Liberal Gazette,* its official organ, argued that the tax would merely "buttress state extravagance," that, if the law were passed, the government would restore public salaries to the predepression level.[16]

The Ceylonese semi-Gladstonians did not, however, form a tightly knit or completely consistent voting bloc. Thus, W. A. de Silva favored the introduction of an income tax; and E. W. Perera, after opposing tariffs for many years, finally concluded that "one of the articles in the creed of Free Trade is that there is nothing to prevent nascent industries being protected. . . ."[17] By the late 1930's old-style liberalism had largely vanished.

SOCIALISM AND SOCIAL REFORM

Just as old-style liberalism waned, so various social philosophies to the Left became more popular during the nineteen twenties and thirties. But welfare-statist and socialist opinion had few representatives among Ceylonese legislators during this period. As has been mentioned, statutes included such paternalistic measures as the provision of work relief and the establishment of plantation wages boards, but these were deviations from an essentially conservative interventionism rather than endorsements of a "New Dealish" or socialist political philosophy. Within the Legislative Council of 1921-31 perhaps the most nearly Leftist speeches were those of I. X. Pereira, a Ceylonese Indian advocating reformist labor legislation, and C. E. Corea, who stressed the Sinhalese peasants' plight.[18]

After the new constitution introduced adult suffrage to the country, voters elected a few Fabians, "planners," and Marxists to the State Council, but the number remained small. During 1931-35 the "Left" consisted of A. E. Goonesinha, head of the tiny Ceylon Labour party, S. W. R. D. Bandaranaike, who from time to time endorsed a vague and flexible "socialism," D. J. Wimalasurendra, an engineer advocate of "planning," and S. A. Wickremasinghe, who later became head of the island's Communist party but in

---

[15] *Leg., 1919,* p. 69.
[16] *Liberal Gazette,* Dec. 24, 1931, p. 3.
[17] *State, 1931,* pp. 435-40; *1934,* p. 1226.
[18] See *Leg., 1922,* pp. 259-65, 421; *1923,* pp. 311-16; *1926,* pp. 1449-59.

the early 1930's placed his major stress on unemployment relief and social insurance.[19]   The 1936 elections returned Goonesinha and Bandaranaike, whose socialism had become even more flexible, to the Council and added N. M. Perera and D. P. R. Gunawardena, of the newly formed semi-Marxist Lanka Sama Samaja party.[20]

Before the 1930's literary Leftism also was comparatively rare and was largely that of future legislators.   In 1920 Goonesinha's short-lived *Nation* declared: "Ground down by the yoke of Capital for ages, the labourer has worked his way up," but concluded rather more mildly, "Trade Unions are essential for the proper guidance and control of the affairs of the workman."[21]   In 1926 Bandaranaike's short-lived *Island Review* published his views on the pre-1914 age and "The New Era:" "Materially it [the pre-1914 period] was an age of rampant capitalism where Bright and Cobden could preach against personal slavery and as fervently uphold a system which consigned their fellow-countrymen to a far worse slavery than that which the Negroes ever suffered. . . . in place of that economic slavery which was the result of capitalism we have the ideal of the equality of all men." But Bandaranaike also did not admire "Bolshevist Russia," which he described as "one of the most sinister and incalculable forces that the modern world has to reckon with."[22]

In 1933 another future legislator contributed to Leftist literature. When N. M. Perera wrote of "Economic Problems of Democracy," however, he sounded more like a guild socialist than the Marxist leader which he later became:

I do not think our legislators are alive to the economic implications of democracy. . . .   If we predicate pluralism . . . we have no alternative but to predicate the abolition of free competition. . . .   The aim of the State must . . . be so to direct the economic forces that the marginal units of the factors of production must be of equal value, and must in comparison with the alternative uses to which the factors can be put be

[19] See *State*, *1931*, pp. 190, 207-09, 484, 504-07, 1367; *1932*, pp. 420-22, 943, 2295-2303, 2550; *1933*, pp. 738-39, 2237-39, 2375-76; *1935*, pp. 26-31, 550-51, 711-12, 1018-19, 1820, 2118-19, 2133-36, 2257, 2451-56.

[20] See *State*, *1936*, pp. 1384-91; *1937*, pp. 621-27; *1938*, p. 470.   Speeches by L. S. S. P. legislator Perera were in general less Leftist than the Manifesto.

[21] *Nation*, March 14, 1920, p. 2.

[22] *Island Review*, April 1, 1926, pp. 19-22.

the highest. . . . the pluralistic state cannot fulfill its obligations without the loyal support of . . . [guild-like] organizations.[23]

In 1935 the Lanka Sama Samaja party, which remained as a unit until the wartime split into majority Trotskyists and minority Communists, published its first Manifesto: "The Fundamental objective of the LSSP is the establishment of a Socialist Society. This necessarily means: (1) The Socialisation of the means of production, distribution and exchange of commodities. (2) The attainment of national independence. (3) The abolition of economic and political inequality and oppression arising from differences of class, race, caste, creed and sex." Among the "immediate demands on behalf of the toiling masses" were child labor laws, free schoolbooks and noonday meals, unemployment insurance for all workers, a minimum wage law covering all workers, "work or maintenance for all in need," factory legislation, rent restriction, slum clearance, national health insurance, more steeply progressive income taxes, and "progressive abolition of all indirect taxation."[24]

In 1939 the LSSP reiterated its demands in *Resurgent Ceylon: A Progressive Journal,* which also hailed the Russian Third Five-Year Plan as a welcome relief in a world of increasing unemployment and grinding poverty.[25] By this time Marxism had gained a wide following among university undergraduates.[26] Plausible reasons for the Leftward trend on the campus are not hard to find. Dreams of a brave new world appealed to young men whose personal ambitions and generous hopes alike seemed to be frustrated by the existing order. Russia's rise from an agricultural, underdeveloped economy excited the same interest and admiration as Japan's rapid progress earlier in the century. In Ceylon, as elsewhere in south Asia, the combination of foreign rule and foreign private investment made Lenin's theory of capitalist imperialism very persuasive, and European Marxists and moderate socialists usually were in the forefront of those demanding independence for colonies.

Meanwhile Father Peter A. Pillai had begun to spell out the Catholic criticisms of, and recommendations for, the social order,

---

[23] *Ceylon Economic Journal,* Dec., 1933, pp. 35-45.

[24] The Manifesto is reprinted in *Sama Samajist,* Aug. 25, 1955.

[25] *Resurgent Ceylon,* March, 1939, pp. 3, 8-10.

[26] See the report of a public debate in the *University College Magazine,* Dec., 1938, pp. 83-87.

interpreting the Papal Encyclicals *Rerum Novarum* and *Quadregesimo Anno* for the Ceylonese. In 1936 *The Social Question* denounced the evils of capitalism, but warned that "Capitalism must not be confounded with every regime that admits private property or even the uses of capital, to which a share of the profits of an enterprise is claimed to be due." The Catholic Church, he continued, "does not desire the abolition of private property, but only asks for its control in the interests of the common good. . . . private ownership alone is capable of harmonizing the requirements of personal liberty with the best use of the material goods of this world. . . . The duty of distributing surplus wealth is an obligation of charity, but it is none the less a strict obligation."[27] The Catholic Social Guild, founded in 1937, favored minimum wage laws and measures to bring about a wide diffusion of property. A 1940 issue of *Social Justice* argued that the government should not only give uncultivated land to landless peasants, but should forcibly purchase farm lands recently acquired by foreign mortgage creditors and divide these also among peasants whose holdings were nonexistent or too small.[28]

In 1939 "Various Medical Men" set forth, in *Ceylon's Uplift*, doctrines similar to Father Pillai's. Buddhist rather than Christian ethics were, however, the basis of their teachings. Ceylon, remarked Dr. B. E. Fernando in his foreword, had a "great need of . . . a set of literature . . . to stem the tide of unhealthy Western influence on our Buddhist culture."[29] Co-operativism was another "middle

[27] *The Social Question* (Colombo: Catholic Social Guild, Nov., 1936), pp. 9-13.

In 1938 the *University College Magazine (loc. cit.)* reported a debate between Father Pillai and a Marxist opponent, the formal resolution being "Distributism is the only true solution for the economic ills of the world." Father Pillai, reported the student Economic Society's Acting Secretary, "rose to speak amidst applause. He began with a violent indictment of the state of society in which we live," eloquently demonstrated the inability of capitalistic governments to remedy the situation, and "next went on to prove the inadequacy of communism as a solution, forgetting that communism was less a solution than a way of life." Balasundram, the Marxist speaker, termed Distributism a return to the Middle Ages, held that History prevented such a backward march, and argued that private property is the root of social troubles. He then, continued the Acting Secretary, "shattered the silly argument that in Russia the individual owned nothing," and eulogized Communism, "which he said gave freedom from economic anxiety." Father Pillai's resolution "was put to the House and defeated by a large majority" who agreed with the views of the Communist speaker.

[28] See the *Social Justice Annual*, 1952, p. 44.

[29] Various Medical Men, *Ceylon's Uplift* (Colombo: Associated Newspapers of Ceylon, 1939), pp. 1-2.

path" proposed between old-style liberalism and statist economics. As early as 1916 a recent Calcutta student, Swami Nathan, published *The Co-operative Movement,* arguing that "despotism or . . . one-man power" was not consistent with economic freedom and had already died in religion, politics, and domestic life and therefore had "no claim to still linger on in the domain of industry and trade." Only producers' co-operativeness, he continued, could put an end to the antagonism between capital and labor. So far most producers' co-operatives had been unsuccessful, because members lacked capital and knowledge. "But the initiative should come from selfless, rich, and philanthropic men."[30]

In 1938 "J .A." wrote even more enthusiastically in *New Ceylon:* "This is our ideology . . . great panacea for all rural ills—'Co-operation'. . . . Co-operation stands in its divine sublimity for the promotion of mutual interests, for the upliftment of the villages, and the economic self-sufficiency of the entire community. . . . Co-operation stands for the moral upliftment of the community."[31]

Intervening articles in the *Ceylon Economic Journal* discussed the past record and possible future functions of co-operative credit societies.[32]   Their authors, however, did not look upon co-operativism as a way of life or a universally applicable method of economic organization, but as an arrangement suitable in special circumstances and worthy of cautious experimentation.   Attitudes expressed in the *Journal* closely resembled those of contemporary policy makers, who did not place much stress on co-operatives.[33]

WORLD WAR II: THE TREND TO THE LEFT

The 1940's in Ceylon saw the swing of conservative interventionism to the Left until it merged with Fabian, co-operativist, and welfare-statist elements under the banner of "practical socialism." In part this was attributable to the pressure of wartime emergencies, which forced the government to play a more active economic role, especially in the production and distribution of foodstuffs.   Japan's

---

[30] Swami Nathan, *The Co-operative Movement* (Jaffna: Sri Sanmuganathan Press, 1916), pp. 1, 8-9.
[31] *New Ceylon,* April, 1938, pp. 2-3.
[32] *Ceylon Economic Journal,* June, 1929, pp. 12-43; Dec., 1934, pp. 2-11.
[33] See *Leg., 1919,* p. 183; *1921,* pp. 39, 64-67; *1926,* pp. 1524-29; *1931,* p. 383; *State, 1932,* pp. 432, 692, 2422, 3321; *1933,* p. 1570; *1935,* p. 220; *1936,* pp. 302-04, 558, 1117; *1938,* pp. 1110-16.

conquest of southeast Asia cut off the usual source of rice imports, and hard-pressed Britain could not supply the shipping for adequate food supplies from the Americas; so self-sufficiency for Ceylon changed from a matter of national pride and economic stability to one of preventing large-scale starvation. The government speeded its program of opening up new food-producing areas, encouraged more intensive cultivation, and forced plantations to grow food for their employees or contribute to a food-production fund. Since imports depended upon British cargo space, the state also assumed responsibility for supplies from overseas, negotiating the quantities and prices with British authorities. When Japan's air attack on Colombo and threatened invasion of Ceylon sent Indian storekeepers back to their homeland, the government added retail distribution to its duties, hurriedly organizing a system of state-financed and supervised co-operative stores. Food subsidies, price controls, rationing, and compulsory deliveries rounded out the list of governmental distributional functions.

Wartime shortages of manufactures were not so critical but were a major handicap to a country that had long since discarded feudal ways of life. These shortages, plus the State Council's growing impatience with a private enterprise that did not push desired industrial programs, led to the decision that the government must itself build and operate a number of factories. The conditions that produced consumer shortages also made it difficult for the Department of Commerce and Industries to secure the necessary industrial equipment and materials, but the Department pushed ahead, using such makeshifts as it could and adhering fairly closely to a schedule of priorities recommended before the emergency.[34]

Initially, the State Council took on its new agricultural, marketing, and industrial roles in a reluctant spirit, approving the new policies only because the government seemed to be the only agency capable of preventing economic chaos.[35] By the end of the war, however, majority opinion had moved so far from its 1940 position as to reserve "basic" manufacturing industries for the state, look

[34] For a record of wartime operation of new factories, see *Report of the Commission on Government Commercial Undertakings*. For a summary of prewar plans, see *Report on Industrial Development and Policy*, p. 6.

[35] See *State, 1940*, pp. 1642, 1651-54; *1943*, pp. 1938-41; *House, 1947-48*, v. 1, c. 2149-50.

upon government-financed and supervised co-operatives as a major element in the economic system, and favor a flexible variety of over-all "planning."[36]   The dominant legislative group also now endorsed free tuition and rapid expansion of schools, free medical services and rapid expansion of hospital facilities, a more systematic and expanded system of work relief and aid for the poor, housing subsidies, and postwar retention of food subsidies, rent controls, and price controls.[37]   Neomercantilism had so transformed itself as hardly to be recognizable.

Political speeches, editorials, and articles are guideposts along the road to conservative interventionism's merger with the moderate Left. Veteran D. S. Senanayake, whose record showed him to be neither a social reformer nor a parlor pink, was the dominant figure in the State Council[38] and was to become the nation's first Prime Minister, but the leading anticapitalist speeches came from his son Dudley and from J. R. Jayewardene, who were to accept prominent positions in the postwar Cabinet. S. W. R. D. Bandaranaike, another prominent Senanayake lieutenant during 1947-51, likewise made socialistic speeches during the war years, thus sounding more like the orator and editor of the 1920's than the Council member of the immediate prewar period.[39]

Outside the State Council perhaps the most significant indication of the Leftward trend was its reflection in organs of business opinion. In 1941 *Ceylon Industrial Development*, published by the Ceylon Chamber of National Industries, stated, "The New Deal of the U. S. A., suited to local conditions, must be our aim."[40]   In 1945 its successor publication, *Ceylon Industrial and Trade Recorder*, ran a series, "Points on Economic Planning," which included such remarks as: ". . . poverty must be abolished if freedom is to be preserved." "The defects of our system are that the legal framework permits as just, an unjust distribution of what is produced."

[36] See *Senate, 1947-48*, c. 15-16; and *Report on Industrial Development and Policy*, pp. 14-20.

[37] See *State, 1946*, c. 2207-23; *Senate, 1947-48*, c. 15-18; and *Post-war Development Proposals* (Colombo: Government Record Office, 1946).

[38] Senanayake replaced the aging D. B. Jayatilaka as Leader of the State Council in late 1942.

[39] See *State, 1943*, pp. 1440-48, 1629; *1944*, pp. 437-40, 465, 650-53; *1945*, c. 3508-11.

[40] *Ceylon Industrial Development*, Jan.-March, 1941, p. 15.

"Planning is necessary because all the world's economists of repute admit and have shown that competitive capitalism has come to the end of its fast expansive era and also that the present economic system cannot ensure Full Employment."[41]

Young Ceylon, one of the island's longer-lived periodicals, also revealed a change in opinion since prewar days. In 1938 it had been sceptical of grandiose programs, but in 1943 it urged, "National Planning for Ceylon must be an ambitious scheme of National foundational planning . . . covering the entire fabric of the life of the people and to plan for Ceylon a new order, politically, economically and internationally."[42] *The Young Writer* warned that government policy must be based upon an essential individualism: ". . . all human progress springs from individual initiative, and . . . the aim of state action should be to create the positive conditions within which every one will be able to make the most and the best of himself in his own way." But even the *Young Writer* favored some varieties of government paternalism: ". . . rural reconstruction must start from the top."[43]

Among academic writings, C. Suriyakumaran's *Ceylon, Beveridge and Bretton Woods* provides an example of the trend. Recently returned from the London School of Economics, the author urged that "neither nationalisation and adaptation nor development can be left entirely to 'free' enterprise," that unemployment was the probable alternative to state-operated factories, and that Russia's Five-Year Plans had illustrated what underdeveloped countries could accomplish.[44] Communist and Trotskyist views appeared in some student writings, also in pamphlets and periodicals issued by noncampus intellectuals.[45] The University of Ceylon's faculty economists, however, expressed less radical opinions than their students. Lecturer K. P. Mukerji expounded a philosophical, non-Marxian socialism.[46] Professor B. B. Das Gupta thought that the government should

[41] *Ceylon Industrial and Trade Recorder,* April, 1945, pp. 8-9; May, 1945, pp. 8-10, 15; July, 1945, pp. 8-9.
[42] *Young Ceylon,* Oct., 1938, pp. 98-99; May-June, 1943, p. 174.
[43] *Young Writer,* Aug., 1942, p. 1; Dec., 1943, p. 2.
[44] C. Suriyakumaran, *Ceylon, Beveridge and Bretton Woods* (Colombo: *Ceylon Daily News,* 1946), pp. 23, 27-28, 37-50, 68.
[45] For an attempt to reconcile Marxist and Buddhist teachings, see Leuke, *Gautama the Buddha and Karl Marx* (Colombo: Vijaya Publishing House, 1943).
[46] K. P. Mukerji, "The Institution of Property," *University of Ceylon Review,* IV (Oct., 1946), 25-33.

finance much of the postwar building for lower-income families, but preferred an essentially private-enterprise system and warned that social services "must not be at the cost of economic development."[47]

FREE CEYLON

THE U. N. P. REGIME: 1947-56

By the time that Ceylon's first Parliament met in late 1947, the merger of conservative interventionism and the moderate Left had taken the political shape of the United National party, which formed the 1947-56 Cabinets and initially commanded the support of most legislators except Communists, Trotskyists, and representatives of Tamil-speaking groups.[48]   Council Leader D. S. Senanayake, whose long public record revealed nationalist and interventionist but not egalitarian sympathies, became the island's first Prime Minister and chose a Cabinet that represented both ideological wings of his party and aimed many of its speeches at low-income and reformist voters.

Parliament's first session marked the high tide of the U. N. P. regime's "practical socialism."   The Governor-General stated in his initial address:

My Government realises that the future well-being of this country depends to a great extent on the sound development of its resources and that the first step in this direction is Planning . . . . Increased production, particularly in the matter of home-grown food will be given a place of supreme importance in the policy of the Government. . . . The establishment of new industrial projects will also engage the serious attention of the Government. . . . A department of Rural Development has been set up . . . (which will) greatly assist economic well-being of the peasantry. . . . The Co-operative Movement, which experienced considerable expansion during the War will be maintained with increased vigor. . . . Another new Department that has been created is the Department of Social Services . . . (to administer) measures which may be decided on. . . .

Specific promises included free education, improvement of medical

[47] B. B. Das Gupta, "Local Authorities and Housing in Ceylon," *University of Ceylon Review*, II (Nov., 1944) 68-76; B. B. Das Gupta, "Some Problems of Social Security," *Ceylon Economic Journal*, XII (Dec., 1946), 56-69.

[48] See W. Ivor Jennings, "The Ceylon General Election of 1947," *University of Ceylon Review*, VI (July, 1948), 133-95.

services, the provision of housing and water, and "Town and Country Planning."[49]

M. D. Banda, one of the back-benchers chosen to comment on the Governor-General's address, continued the general theme and tied "planning," state enterprise, and social services to Ceylon's newly won independence: ". . . political freedom is only a means to greater ends . . . to have any meaning for the masses of this country, [it] must lead to economic and social freedom as well. It must lead to . . . a new order of society . . . based on principles of social justice, giving equal opportunities to all avenues of life." Junior Cabinet member M. S. Kariapper praised U. N. P. policy as "the middle path, constitutional socialism . . . the creed which the democratic countries, particularly Great Britain, have followed with very happy results during the past few years."[50]

Nor was the United National party's "practical socialism" entirely talk. Laws and administrative policies provided free medical services, food subsidies, and housing subsidies; extended or established price controls, rent controls, and wages boards; subsidized and gave various preferences to co-operative enterprise; conferred greater security of tenure on some tenant farmers; promoted, subsidized, and regulated "rural reconstruction" and new peasant farming in the Dry Zone; made the government the sole importer of rice, and reserved all "basic" industries for state enterprise. As defined in 1946, "basic" industries included power, iron and steel, cement, "heavy" chemicals (including fertilizers), certain drugs and pharmaceuticals, and cotton spinning, a rather comprehensive list for little-industrialized Ceylon.[51] "Today," boasted Finance Minister J. R. Jayewardene in July, 1948, "the State can by legislative act control production as well as distribution, decide the location of factories, and compel the employer to attend to the welfare of the workers."[52]

"Practical socialism" was, however, a highly eclectic program and far removed from what the U. N. P.'s opposition understood by the term. Prime Minister D. S. Senanayake resembled Franklin D. Roosevelt of the early New Deal days more closely than he resembled most European socialist leaders when he refused to assign either

[49] *Senate, 1947-48,* c. 15-18.
[50] *House, 1947-48,* v. 1, c. 43, 1181.
[51] See *Report on Industrial Development and Policy,* pp. 16-17.
[52] *House, 1948-49,* v. 3, c. 1046.

minimum or maximum boundaries to the state, approved only pragmatic tests of policies, and spoke of the profit incentive as a force to be harnessed rather than destroyed.[53]   Moreover, the Cabinet's more outspokenly "socialist" members quickly began to lose some of their enthusiasm for generous welfare measures and the whole-sale reconstruction of society.   In the same speech in which he boasted of the government's new powers, Jayewardene argued that Ceylon was too poor to institute a British-type system of social services.   A few days later he argued that, although the government was trying "to alter the broad framework of our social and economic structure," state enterprise was not a panacea: ". . . the profit motive is only one of the motives that actuate man.   If you remove the profit motive, some other motive will take its place.   In the Soviet Union, the mo-tive for power has reared its ugly head. . . ."   Furthermore, ". . . nationalisation requires a high sense of duty and discipline which the hon. Members of the Marxist group are daily trying to undermine by their misinterpretation of Marxist philosophy."[54] Minister of Agricul-ture Dudley Senanayake likewise expressed, in 1948, sentiments rather different from those of wartime speeches, now contending that the Opposition used the word "monopoly" much too loosely and that all-pervading state ownership would be far worse than monopoly capitalism.   "We prefer the path of economic freedom. . . ."[55]

Parliament enacted some new statist and welfare legislation during 1949-52,[56] filling gaps in the program set forth in earlier speeches. In general, however, there was a slow movement away from egalita-rian measures and state enterprise, as the Cabinet began to place greater stress upon financial and other difficulties.   In 1953 the foreign-exchange shortage following the Korean War led to a drastic slash in food subsidies and even greater emphasis on finances.   Dur-ing the same year the International Bank Mission's report, *The Economic Development of Ceylon,* and the *Report of the Commis-sion on Government Commercial Undertakings* set in motion a funda-mental debate on the roles of the state, domestic private enterprise,

[53] *House, 1947-48,* v. 2, c. 2825-26; *1948-49,* v. 5, c. 2188-89; *1950-51,* v. 9, c. 1923.
[54] *House, 1948-49,* v. 3, c. 1052-53, 1853-61.
[55] *House, 1948-49,* v. 3, c. 1555.
[56] E. g., a Paddy Lands Act to give tenants greater security of tenure, a soil conservation act, acts to reorganize existing government factories.

and foreign capital.[57]   Unpaid debts and generally disappointing records also made the Cabinet lose much of the faith earlier expressed in the co-operative movement.   By 1955 U. N. P. policy had retreated so far from "practical socialism" as to resemble the conservative interventionism of the late 1930's about as closely as it did the bold ideas of 1947-48.

Among the signs of change was the U. N. P.'s less frequent use of the word "planning."   In 1948, when Finance Minister J. R. Jayewardene described his anticipated projects, he spoke of a "Six-Year Plan."   In 1955, when his successor and namesake M. D. H. Jayawardene made known his proposed schedule, he called it a "Six-Year Programme of Investment."   "Socialism" was another term that enjoyed less Cabinet favor than in earlier years, especially in discussions of industrial policy.   Here the change was substantive as well as semantic.   In 1948 Minister C. Sittampalam prefaced a policy speech by saying that, since the government was "socialist," "we must not make use of private capital to make money out of the labour of this country if we can do it ourselves."   He then apologetically added, ". . . it may be that, in the case of certain industries, private enterprise might be in a better position to implement the industrialization policy than Government."   Six years later Minister K. Vaithianathan expressed a quite different attitude when he described the Cabinet's new policy: ". . . the first duty of Government is not to do things for which it is not well equipped . . . if Government creates a favourable climate and provides fertile soil, the innate urges, talents and ambitions of the individual in Ceylon would be given fullest play, and the resultant production would exceed many-fold anything the Government could help to produce direct."[58]

As the Planning Secretariat put it, "Industrialisation in the programme is based on a new policy designed to help the private sector to help itself."   The government, however, did not intend quickly to relinquish all its manufacturing enterprises or even to cease starting new ones.   Rather, the scheme called for partnership between state and private enterprise, with the former assuming certain initial

[57] *House, 1952-53,* v. 13, c. 3026-79; *1954-55,* v. 19, c. 2035-39, 2062; v. 20, c. 1806-07, 1842-43, 3654-3727; *Senate, 1954-55,* v. 8, c. 366-98, 661-86.
[58] *House, 1948-49,* v. 4, c. 1321; *Senate, 1954-55,* v. 8, c. 672.

risks and the latter taking over the factories' operation at some later date. Among the agencies created under the program were the Institute of Scientific and Industrial Research, to provide technical assistance to new and established industry, and the Development Finance Corporation, to provide both loan and share capital.[59]

The Planning Secretariat's 1955 remarks on the co-operative movement show that, with respect to this "middle path" as well as to state enterprise, the U. N. P. now took a middle position:

Co-operation has a particularly important role to play in our economy in its present state of development . . . in his co-operative he [the small "traditional" producer] remains master of his own destiny and preserves most of his cherished social values. . . . he can combine modern enterprise with his moral values of self-help and mutual help. The co-operative way . . . has to be promoted and preserved, using it to give the members not only a higher annual income but also a greater degree of leisure due to a rise in his productivity. [But] The Co-operative movement has already taken such a hold on the minds of the community that it is sometimes regarded as a panacea. . . . there are 77 varieties of societies. . . .This rapid expansion has had some unfortunate repercussions on the Movement. The standards of bookkeeping and honesty are not as high as they ought to be. The Movement should concentrate on improving the quality more than on increasing the number of societies. . . . For the Movement to flourish, all those who are working in it must be fully conversant with co-operative principles and ideas. . . . Past experience has shown that the pace of the Movement should not be forced unless trained persons are available to man the Co-operative Societies as office-bearers and employees.[60]

The Cabinet had, several years before 1955, already ceased to talk of an ambitious social-insurance program. The Planning Secretariat apparently summed up their position when it remarked, of public expenditures in general: "Programmes prepared exclusively on the basis of needs without reference to resources are likely, in the last analysis, to prove illusory. Countries which are in the fortunate position of being able to satisfy all their needs are not, by definition, poor."[61] The rising cost of education likewise caused

[59] *Six-Year Programme of Investment, 1954-55 to 1959-60* (Colombo, 1955), pp. 28, 237-45.
[60] *Ibid.*, pp. 217-19.
[61] *Ibid.*, pp. 14, 426.

alarm in government circles.[62] Competitive examinations were employed to slow expanding enrollment in secondary schools, and some public officials proposed that a similar hurdle be introduced at still an earlier year. Only with respect to agricultural expansion, rural reconstruction, and protectionism did the U. N. P.'s 1955 economic policies closely resemble those preached in the first flush of Ceylon's independence. These were also areas in which 1947 proposals did not differ greatly from the ambitions that prewar conservative interventionists had cherished.

THE OPPOSITION AND THE NEW REGIME

During the first few years of Parliamentary government, the leading opposition to the United National Party came from the Marxist Left, descendants of the prewar Lanka Sama Samaja party, who captured nearly a quarter of the seats in the 1947 election.[63] The Marxists did not, however, unite into one political party. During the war the L. S. S. P. had split into two wings, a Communist minority favoring support of Britain after the Nazi invasion of Russia, and a largely Trotskyist majority denouncing the war as a struggle among rival imperialists. This division continued after the war, and the majority, retaining the Lanka Sama Samaja name, in turn split into factions.

Ceylon's Communist party appears to be a branch of the international movement directed from Moscow and has strong emotional attachments, at least, to the Peking regime. Its long-run program stresses nationalization without compensation, industrial development, and close ties with the Communist world. When debating current policies, its spokesmen have denounced the United National party as tools of Western economic imperialists and have called for more restrictions on Western capital, more generous social services and subsidies to the poor, more freedom of action for unions, and heavy emphasis upon state industrial enterprise.[64]

[62] See *House, 1950-51*, v. 9, c. 270-72; *1952-53*, v. 12, c. 3719-42; E. B. Tisseverasinghe, "The Pattern of Occupation in Idealized Ceylon," *New Lanka*, Vol. VI (Jan., 1955), esp. pp. 51, 57.

[63] See W. Ivor Jennings, "The Ceylon General Election of 1947," *University of Ceylon Review*, VI (July, 1948), 133-195; I. D. S. Weerawardana, "The General Election in Ceylon, 1952," *Ceylon Historical Journal*, II (July-Oct., 1952), 109-78.

[64] Communist party leader S. A. Wickremasinghe has proposed an economic program in *The Way Ahead* (Colombo: Lanka Press, 1955). Also see speeches by

Non-Communist heirs of the prewar Lanka Sama Samaja party retained the old name but soon split into factions whose relationships among one another have been rather complicated. During Parliament's first session the division was between a majority wing, led by N. M. Perera and usually termed the L. S. S. P., and a minority wing led by Colvin R. de Silva and usually called the Bolshevik-Leninist party. Shortly thereafter Perera and De Silva combined to form what Ceylonese now call the "Nava" (or new) L. S. S. P., but a substantial fraction of the former majority group, under the leadership of Philip Gunawardena, refused to join this combination and became the Viplavakari L. S. S. P. In 1952 the V. L. S. S. P. formed an election alliance with the Communists, but a little later they severed this connection also, remaining a small, unaffiliated party until shortly before the 1956 elections, when they coalesced with the less Leftist, Sinhalese-stressing Sri Lanka Freedom party. Several prominent former members of the Nava Lanka Sama Samaja party and a few former Communists also joined the coalition, without first enlisting in the Viplavakari L. S. S. P.[65]

Because of all these splits, coalitions, and defections, and because of substantial differences of opinion among supporters of the largest (or Perera-led) wing, it is difficult to summarize L. S. S. P. opinion. In general, before the 1956 realignments all leaders endorsed about the same long-run economic program as the Communists. The Nava L. S. S. P. still proclaims itself to be Trotskyist and publishes articles on and by the Fourth International's revered leader.[66] A large fraction of its following, however, has consisted of men whose views are closer to Western social democrats,[67] and some support

P. Keuneman and Mrs. D. Wickremasinghe, *House, 1951-52*, v. 10, c. 217; *1952-53*, v. 13, c. 1833-42, 2349-67; *1953-54*, v. 14, c. 1834-46; v. 15, c. 1717; *1954-55*, v. 18, c. 702-10, 1313-37.

[65] Many of these joined the short-lived Samasta Lanka Sinhala Basha Peramuna, under the leadership of former N. L. S. S. P. legislator W. Dahanayake, who became Minister of Education in the new 1956 Cabinet. Dahanayake joined the S. L. F. P. after the election.

[66] See their weekly newspaper, the *Sama Samajist.*

[67] Some Ceylonese believe that there are substantial differences of opinion among the party's leaders, with N. M. Perera being essentially a social democrat and Colvin R. de Silva holding essentially Trotskyist views. Perera's speeches in the *House of Representatives* have usually been less doctrinaire than De Silva's and most of his speeches in the prewar State Council did not sound very Marxist. For some of their more comprehensive postwar speeches, see *House, 1947-48*, v. 1, c. 916-951; *1948-49*, v. 3, c. 1558-1594, 1798-1834; *1949-50*, v. 6, c. 1269-

has come from voters who have regarded the N. L. S. S. P., in spite of Trotskyist affiliations, as more militantly nationalist than the United National party and more genuinely nationalist than the Communists.[68] Many Ceylonese adherents of other parties believe that, should the Trotskyists somehow gain power, their economic program as well as their political procedures would be much more moderate than their Communist rivals'.

The Parliamentary Opposition also initially included the Ceylon Indian Congress and the Tamil Congress. The former chiefly represented Indian plantation workers and preached social reformist and Fabian doctrines.[69] After the election of 1952 they ceased to exist as a legislative group, since by that time most Ceylon Indians had been disfranchised. The Tamil Congress represented the Tamil-speaking folk of northern and eastern Ceylon, who distrusted the U. N. P. as a Sinhalese-dominated party. By 1949, however, the Congress leader had accepted a major Cabinet post and the Congress itself had virtually merged with its erstwhile foe. Those Tamils who continued to doubt the U. N. P.'s intentions continued their opposition as the Tamil Federalist party. Tamil legislators have not differed greatly from the U. N. P. in their views concerning the proper economic role of the state.

During the last several years of the U. N. P. regime the largest segment of the Opposition was the Sri Lanka Freedom party, formed and headed by S. W. R. D. Bandaranaike, who left the Cabinet in 1951.[70] Policy differences between the Cabinet and the new party did not concern domestic economic policy so much as Ceylon's economic and political relationships with Western powers and the

---

1340; *1950-51*, v. 8, c. 1184-99; *1951-52*, v. 10, c. 1603-41; *1953-54*, v. 14, c. 913-84; *1954-55*, v. 18, c. 346-98; v. 20, c. 3662-75; *1955-56*, v. 21, c. 978-1021. Also see N. M. Perera, "Some Observations on the Colombo Plan," *Ceylon Economist*, Vol. I (Feb., 1951), 289-93. De Silva has contributed many short Trotskyist articles to *Sama Samajist*.

[68] During the Second World War, the L. S. S. P., like the Congress party in India, opposed participation in the war or aid to Britain. The Communists favored participation after the Nazi attack on Russia.

[69] See the speeches by G. R. Motha, *House*, *1947-48*, v. 2, c. 2568-70; *1948-49*, v. 3, c. 93, 202-03, 1342-63. Motha and other spokesmen were, however, men of property, whose chief ties with the plantation laborers were those of "community."

[70] Bandaranaike stated that he left the Cabinet because the U. N. P. would not rapidly replace English with Sinhalese and Tamil as the official languages. Critics argued that he formed a new party because he despaired of succeeding D. S. Senanayake as head of the U. N. P.

stress to be placed upon the Sinhalese language and traditions.[71] The S. L. F. P. attached much less value to ties with and prospective aid from the West, and wished to a greater extent to subordinate other groups' interests to those of the Sinhalese community.

Nevertheless, the economic program which the S. L. F. P. favored in resolutions and speeches was well to the Left of that endorsed by the post-1951 United National party. The most dramatic differences concerned the degree of nationalization desired. It was not clear to what extent the new party merely favored nationalization "in principle" and to what extent it proposed government seizure in the near future, but part of a 1951 manifesto read: "All essential services including large plantations and transport, banking and insurance [should] be progressively nationalised. This is the necessary corollary of the policy of taxing high incomes and the control of the accumulation of too much private capital, without which industry must collapse."[72]   The S. L. F. P. differed from the Marxist parties, however, in that it proposed to compensate dispossessed owners.

Again unlike the Marxists, the Sri Lanka Freedom party put first emphasis upon agricultural output and Sinhalese peasants' problems, rather than upon industrial growth. Early in 1956 a party spokesman wrote: "Unlike the U. N. P.'s haphazard agricultural schemes the S. L. F. P. envisages schemes based on peasant co-operation and large settlements with emphasis on self-help. Much as the methods used in China are detested, careful study will be made of collectivisation in agriculture which has been an integral part of the successful progress of Chinese economic development plans."[73]   Among measures for which S. L. F. P. legislators asked were expansion of villages' cultivable areas, laws to confer greater security of tenure upon tenants, and steps to vacate Indian plantation workers from their jobs, so as to make room for landless and underemployed Sinhalese. The new party also asked that estate taxes be made so high as to be "prohibitive" (in order that "capital may not pass into the hands of persons who have done nothing to earn or accumulate same") and asked for a more bountiful social service program. Bandaranaike rebuked his

[71] Bandaranaike's initial demand was that Sinhalese and Tamil replace English. By late 1955 the cry had become "Sinhalese only!"
[72] See the S. L. F. P. weekly newspaper *Free Lanka*, Jan. 8, 1956, p. 3.
[73] *Ibid., loc. cit.*

former colleagues for slashing the rice subsidy and withdrawing free meals for school children during the 1953 exchange crisis.[74]

Early in 1956 the S. L. F. P. formed an election alliance, termed the People's United Front, with the Viplavakari Lanka Sama Samaja party and various other Leftist dissidents who had withdrawn from the Nava L. S. S. P. and the Communist party. The coalition, in which the S. L. F. P. greatly outnumbered its new allies, drew up a platform resembling the Freedom party's previous demands.[75] Among paragraphs dealing with economic policies were:

5. National Planning and Taxation: We shall give top priority to the preparation of a real plan for development as well as social services, and recast our taxation system according to the needs of that plan, relieving the poor and the middle classes from the burden that now falls on them, particularly by the taxation of necessaries, and by adjusting the other taxes in a manner that will ensure the greatest possible stimulus to economic developments. The cost of living will be reduced by lowering the price of necessaries like rice and sugar and by re-consideration of the present policy of rationing.

8. Housing: While assistance is given to private enterprise, the State must accept primary responsibility for this service. . . .and the necessary financial provision for this purpose must be made. . . .priorities must be fixed for different classes of buildings, top priority being given to residences necessary for the people.

9. Social Services: We shall immediately introduce health and un-employment insurance and old-age pensions. . . .

10. Agriculture and Land Development: . . . The needs of the landless peasant will be effectively provided for by village expansion schemes . . . and by colonization schemes in which the ownership of the land will be vested in the peasant, and all necessary assistance given to them by the State until the land is developed.

11. Industries: All key industries must be run by the State. Small industries such as cottage industries can be in the hands of private enterprise. Priority must be given to agricultural industries such as paddy, cotton, and sugar-cane and such other industries as sugar, textiles, fisheries, salt and fertilizers.

[74] For legislative speeches presenting S. L. F. P. views, see *House*, *1952-53*, v. 12, c. 1356-58, 1558-72, 1758-85, 3849-50, v. 13, c. 265; *1953-54*, v. 15, c. 200, 390-91, 995-96; *1954-55*, v. 18, c. 1039-1056, 1074-98, 1365-88, v. 19, c. 54.

[75] *Free Lanka*, March 11, 1956, p. 3.

19. Nationalisation: All essential industries, including foreign-owned plantations, transport, banking and insurance, will be progressively nationalised.

Except for the paragraph concerning land development, the platform called for measures of a more statist and/or egalitarian nature than recent U. N. P. policy. During the election campaign, however, the People's United Front did not pay nearly as much attention to its economic proposals as to its championship of Sinhalese language and culture, and numerous sceptics remained unconvinced that a Bandaranaike-led Cabinet would push through nearly so ambitious a program. There was much talk that many of the proposed economic policies would never advance beyond campaign oratory and that the alliance between the S. L. F. P. and the former Trotskyists could not long survive the election. When the People's United Front won a two-thirds majority in Parliament and the U. N. P. elected fewer legislators than the Nava L. S. S. P., there were many predictions that the next election fight would be between the S. L. F. P. and a Leftist coalition.[76]

The eight months following the election have been too short a period to indicate how greatly the new regime will alter Ceylon's economic policies. Some leading Cabinet members come from the former Trotskyites' ranks, and spokesmen for the ruling coalition have announced their intention to push through the promised program. The Cabinet has instructed a National Planning Council to draw up a comprehensive, long-term plan co-ordinating development in all lines of economy, including the private as well as the public.[77] Much of the talk, however, does not differ greatly form that coming from the U. N. P. Cabinet in the early days of its "practical socialism." It is too early to know what "planning" will mean.

Significant measures in the 1956 program of the People's United Front include a subsidized slash in the price of rice, higher taxes on individual and company incomes and estates, and trade agreements

[76] These predictions were made in spite of the fact that the U. N. P. received about twice as large a popular vote as the N. L. S. S. P. and the Communists combined. The prophets looked forward to a continuing Left trend. In late 1956, however, the trend was at least temporarily reversed. Municipal elections showed strong gains for the U. N. P. at the expense of both the People's United Front and the Marxist Left.

[77] See *Ceylon News*, Nov. 1, 1956, pp. 9, 16. The editorial on p. 16 questions the Council's ability to perform its assigned duties.

with Eastern European countries. Preliminary steps have been taken for the nationalization of bus lines, and various reports indicate that very probably the new Cabinet has reversed the trend towards private enterprise in manufacturing. To date, however, the Bandaranaike regime has not appeared impatient to begin large-scale transformation of the economy, and the implication of many statements and actions is that the Cabinet will study the problems involved in various parts of their pre-election program and decide later whether the promised policies are feasible. Ambitious nationalization of foreign properties especially seems to have receded into a shadowy future.[78]

ACADEMIC AND JOURNALISTIC OPINION

If academic opinion wields much influence, the trend in Ceylon's economic policies will be at least as statist and egalitarian as the new regime has promised. Marxism has long been intellectually fashionable among university students; a majority of undergraduates call themselves Trotskyists or Communists.[79] Faculty social scientists, while supporting several parties, have been mostly to the Left of the U. N. P. Several faculty members (social science and other) have been active workers for the Nava Lanka Sama Samaja party.

Among academic expressions of opinion have been book reviews and articles in the *University of Ceylon Review*. Several reveal much discontent with the existing economic system. F. R. J. thought that American economist D. M. Wright failed to state the true issue facing a world which must reject "outdated capitalism," that issue being "State Socialism vs. a more truly Democratic Socialism in which workers play an effective part in making the crucial decisions both as regards wages and management."[80] N. K. S. found in a book on socialist pricing "weighty reasons which convince the reader about the superiority of the planned system."[81] Ralph Pieris looked back at an earlier Ceylon and deplored capitalism's unleashing of "those

---

[78] See *Ceylon News*, May 3, 1956, p. 9; May 24, 1956, p. 7; July 19, 1956, p. 16; Sept. 13, 1956, p. 16; Oct. 25, 1956, p. 20.

[79] But apparently most student Leftists have become more conservative after graduation, and the party label frequently has little significance on the campus. Thus, "Rightists" and Communists have formed coalitions to oppose Trotskyist candidates for student office. During 1955-56 there appeared to be some movement away from the Marxist parties to the S. L. F. P.

[80] *University of Ceylon Review* (book review), VII (Oct. 1949), 329-31.

[81] *Ibid.* (book review), VII (Oct., 1949), 328-29.

selfish and avaricious impulses which Buddhism expressly strove to sublimate."[82]   B. B. Das Gupta was less discontented and expressed a distrust of uninformed reformism, pointing out that the co-operative movement, for which such high hopes had been held, had shown rather disappointing results in India.[83]

The *Ceylon Economist* published both scholarly and semipopular articles and notes contributed by both academic and other writers. Perhaps a majority of the contributors were well to the Left in the island's politics.   Before 1954 most of the brief, unsigned notes appeared to be Leninist.   Among the authors of lengthier papers were Nava L. S. S. P. leader N. M. Perera, who attacked the Colombo Plan as a program of international finance-capitalism;[84] Communist party head S. A. Wickremasinghe, who denounced the island's major irrigation project as a surrender to "imperialist vested interests';[85] and economist G. V. S. de Silva, who poured Communist scorn upon the International Bank Mission's report, *The Economic Development of Ceylon.*[86]   Economist N. K. Sarkar argued that Russian experience had shown that planned government enterprise could simultaneously raise consumption and rapidly increase investment in an underdeveloped economy.[87]

But many contributors to the *Ceylon Economist* belonged to the Right and Center.   Banker C. Loganathan deplored high taxes, inadequate protection, and inadequate credit for Ceylonese business.[88] Economist Gamani Corea pointed to administrative, technical, and sociological lacks hampering central planning.[89]   Economist J. B. Kelegama endorsed features of the Cabinet's 1954 industrial policy, pointing out that government factories in Ceylon had a poor record and arguing the need for a "development corporation" to aid

[82] "Sociology and Ideology in Ceylon during a 'Time of Troubles,' 1795-1850," *ibid.,* IX (July, 1951), 171-85.
[83] *Ibid.* (book review), IX (Jan., 1951), 76-77.
[84] N. M. Perera, "Some Observations on the Colombo Plan," *Ceylon Economist,* I (Feb., 1951), 289-93.
[85] S. A. Wickremasinghe, "The Gal Oya Project and the Crisis in Agriculture," *ibid.,* I (June, 1951), 358-74.
[86] G. V. S. de Silva, "The World Bank Mission's Report," *ibid.,* II (Third Quarter, 1952), 207-31.
[87] N. K. Sarkar, "The Budget Debate," *ibid.,* II (Sept., 1951), 102-110.
[88] C. Loganathan, "Some Problems of the Ceylon Economy," *ibid.,* II (Second Quarter, 1952), 102-110.
[89] Gamani Corea, "Some Problems of Economic Development in Ceylon," *ibid.,* I (Aug., 1950), 39-45.

private enterprise and show the way.[90]   With respect to peasant
agriculture, Kelegama asked for such reforms as changes in terms
of tenancy and the end of absentee landlordism; he saw little hope
of major progress through development societies and co-operatives.[91]

Nonacademic periodicals also displayed a wide variety of viewpoints, ranging from conservative interventionism to Leninism,
through a varied middle ground including Catholic, Buddhist, and
other reformism and social democracy.   The periodicals of 1947-56
did not, like those of the immediately preceding years, reflect a
strong over-all trend in opinion but revealed familiar viewpoints and
repeated earlier arguments.

The *Ceylon Journal of Industry and Commerce* occupied a position to the Right of the U. N. P., making far fewer concessions to
egalitarian sentiment and statist views than had preceding organs of
business opinion.   Issue after issue called upon the government to
protect Ceylon businessmen from foreign goods and foreign capital,
and also to give more positive aid and to decrease the extent of governmental control.   Of income redistribution and planning there was
scarcely a word, save for attacks on high taxes and other government
measures said to decrease incentive and reduce capital formation.

Among periodicals advocating a "middle path," the short-lived
Third Force is of some interest because of its apparent relationship
to supporters of the later-appearing Sri Lanka Freedom party.
Calling itself the "Voice of a Centre Democratic Group," *Third
Force* repudiated "the doctrine of Proletarianism as well as the
exploitation of the worker by the capitalist" and called for the "break-
up of existing monopolies and the formation instead of public corporations; joint ownership of all major production—distribution and
transport—industries by the workers (in these instances) and the
general public."[92]

As another part of the Ceylonese Center, the Catholic Social
Guild continued to plead for a reformist, distributivist policy.   Writing in *Social Justice*, Ignatius Gamlath endorsed "Sharing Management with Employees": "We need a society in which the control

[90] J. B. Kelegama, "A Development Corporation for Ceylon," *ibid.*, III (Sept.,
1954), 38-49.
[91] J. B. Kelegama, "The Kandyan Peasantry Problem," *ibid.*, II (Third Quarter,
1952), 181-93, and II (July, 1953), 264-76.
[92] *Third Force*, Feb., 1949, pp. 1-3.

of economic life is exercised by as many people as possible. This
is economic democracy in the wide sense of the word . . . , this
system . . . seems to be a step forward towards the establishment of
an organic economic society, in which alone social peace and harmony,
the fruits of Social Justice, could be realized."[93]   Father B. W. J.
Thasan, writing on *What Is Wrong with the World*, expanded the
ideal of shared management to the dream of a corporate, co-operative
state, featured by town corporations, provincial councils, and a national co-operative chamber. Within this society, each is to enjoy
a status decided by function.[94]

Among Buddhist-inspired politico-economic writings, the most
ambitious was D. C. Vijayavardhana's *Revolt in the Temple*, an
explicit attempt to interpret Buddha's message for contemporary Ceylon. Much of the book is a blast against the West and reflects the
highly emotional Buddhism and Sinhalism which erupted in the
1956 election. Nevertheless, the author regarded J. S. Mill's
Liberty as "the best expression ever given to the reasoned idea of
individual freedom, enjoyed in association with one's fellows,"
and his ideals and policy conclusions differed little from those of
many Western social reformers. Communism's philosophy and
morality have certain similarities with Buddhism, he argued, but
Russian Communism does not show, and Marxist methods cannot
bring about, a tendency towards communal living or equal sharing.
Moreover, while well-meaning reformers seem to aim only at
equality and a comfortable life, men wish to experience difficulties
which "elicit their powers." The modern state, Vijayavardhana
continued, is, like property in land, an enemy of liberty. Co-
operatives appeal to those persons who see the need for change but
do not like the methods and results of revolution.[95]

If the Sinhalese revival continues in full strength, Ceylon is
likely to produce in the near future a more voluminous economic
literature attempting to interpret Buddhist doctrine and asking for
the preservation or recapture of admired aspects of traditional social

[93] Ignatius Gamlath, "Sharing Management with Employees," *Social Justice*,
Nov., 1953, pp. 8-9.
[94] B. W. J. Thasan, *What Is Wrong with the World?* (1948). See especially
the section (pp. 26-29) on "The Co-operative State."
[95] D. C. Vijayavardhana, *The Revolt in the Temple* (Quoted phrases are from
p. 484 and p. 209 respectively).

life. Since the Buddhist sages were not in large part concerned with the problems of a modern exchange economy, and since Sinhalese traditions stem from an agrarian, feudal, caste-dominated Ceylon, the interpreters will probably borrow heavily from Western thought. But the spirit of Sinhalese economic philosophy may differ substantially from that of dominant Western teachings.

4

Economic Development:

I. Agricultural, Industrial, and Financial Policy

CEYLON IS very largely an agricultural economy. The 1946 Census recorded more than half of the island's gainfully employed in "agricultural and related occupations," less than 10 per cent as "craftsmen and production process workers."[1] Most of these latter were not factory employees. Today's statistical picture cannot be greatly different; in the intervening ten years, industrial employment cannot have advanced much more rapidly than the island's population, which is believed to have increased by about one-third during the post-1946 decade.

AGRICULTURE AND MANUFACTURING IN THE CEYLONESE ECONOMY

The fact that Ceylon is so largely agricultural has caused much of the talk of economic development to stress manufacturing industries. Demand for industrialization has been insistent, although of frequently varying strength, for at least forty years, since the time when the First World War interrupted the normal flow of supplies and the colonial Governor appointed a commission to study the island's industrial potentialities. Chapter 2, on "Nationalism and Economics," has already discussed this demand, which has in large part been attributable to nationalist emotions as well as to economic beliefs. Since 1930 unemployment and underemployment also have been major causes of demands for industrial growth. But probably the major reason for Ceylonese spokesmen's emphasis on industrialization, from 1916 to the present time, has been a belief that only through expanded manufacturing can Ceylon achieve a substantially

---

[1] These "production process workers" do not include tea factory and rubber mill employees, who are classified as plantation and therefore agricultural workers. But adjustment for this would not greatly alter the picture.

higher income. This belief, in turn, seems to have been attributable in part to the observed association between manufacturing and high incomes in other countries, in part to more sophisticated economic calculation.

Since so much of the talk has concerned industrial growth, a history of Ceylonese development policies might be expected to show a similarly great emphasis on manufactures. But what the record shows, rather consistently, is a much greater governmental concentration on agricultural than industrial problems. Manufacturing projects have received only a quite small fraction of total government outlay on economic projects, and this is not fully explainable by official reliance on private enterprise to develop industry. During the 1940's, at least, government did not expect private capital to undertake most new manufacturing investment; yet in that decade also the bulk of government "economic" expenditure was on agriculture.

Critics of government policy argue that the high ratio of agricultural to industrial outlay has represented a deliberate attempt to slow manufacturing growth, first by a colonial government determined to keep Ceylon a market for British exports and a source of cheap raw materials, next by a Ceylonese-planter government allied with British capitalists and anxious to preserve the planters' economic and political dominance on the island. Friends of government policy instead explain the agricultural and industrial budgets by a reference to the island's resources and potential markets; greater outlays on manufacturing would, they argue, have been uneconomical.

In any case, the agricultural emphasis has continued, regardless of constitutional and other political changes, from the days of colonial government through two State Councils and at least two Parliaments. Nor does it appear that the People's United Front will alter policy in this respect. Although one wing of the Cabinet consists of former Trotskyists who have long stressed manufacturing, the party's greatest strength lies in the rural areas, and their leading pronouncements have assigned priority to agricultural expansion and reform.

The table below shows expenditures under the "six-year plan" for 1947-53 and the proposed budgetary outlays under the now discarded "six-year programme" for 1954-60, which the U. N. P. Cabinet drew up some months before it lost the 1956 election.

	SIX-YEAR PLAN[2] 1947-53*	SIX-YEAR PROGRAMME,[3] 1954-60*
TOTAL DEVELOPMENT OUTLAY........	1,246.4	2,528
Agriculture, Fisheries and Forestry[4]....	518.8	923
Transport and Communications........	302.4	546
Fuel and Power.....................	74.2	292
Industry...........................	65.4	112
Other..............................	285.6	655

* Millions of rupees

AGRICULTURAL DEVELOPMENT POLICY

From the middle of the nineteenth century the colonial government took various steps to transform Ceylon's economy: the waste lands acts and related land sales which were the foundation of subsequent plantation agriculture, the building and maintenance of roads, the improvement of harbor facilities, the financing of agricultural research, the spread of government hospitals and schools, and so on. In general, the policy had been to encourage private enterprise to develop commercial agriculture and related lines of trade, but to limit encouragement to the provision of a favorable "climate of enterprise" not characterized by protective tariffs, direct subsidies, and major use of government loans.

Until the middle 1920's the world market for Ceylon's exports was such that private capital eagerly took advantage of agricultural opportunities. Coffee, the first major money winner, was struck by disease and vanished during the late nineteenth century, but British planters turned to tea, rubber, and minor crops, while Ceylonese entrepreneurs developed coconut growing, so that by World War I commercial acreage was greater than at the height of the coffee boom. Ceylon's peasants also greatly expanded the area under cultivation. Estimated total acreage in 1931 was nearly eight times as great as that believed to have been cultivated in 1830, so that, al-

[2] *Report of the Taxation Commission* (Sessional Paper XVII, 1955), p. 23.
[3] Planning Secretariat, *Six-Year Programme of Investment, 1954-55 to 1959-60*, p. 32.
[4] This figure does not include outlay on "rural development and village works," which was set at Rs. 57.6 million in the Six-Year Programme. Outlay on forestry and fisheries is a small part of the whole.

though population rose to more than five times the 1830 figure, farm acreage per head increased by nearly one-half.[5] After 1925, however, export prices fell and commercial agriculture was not profitable enough to encourage substantial expansion. Since the village population continued to increase, peasant farm acreage still rose, but the villages shortly began to press upon boundaries set by rainfall, terrain, and the plantations. Cultivated area per head began the slow decline that has continued until the present.[6]

Even before agricultural depression hit the island, the colonial government began to reconsider its older policy of selling crown lands (seized under the waste lands ordinances) to the highest bidder. Peasants disliked the practice because they could not compete against British planters and Ceylonese of means. Nationalists denounced the land sales as a foreign government's auction of a Ceylonese national asset, often to foreign buyers who brought in foreign labor. After 1916 the government no longer sold plots larger than 10 acres, except in a few special instances. In 1927 it appointed a Land Commission to advise concerning a possible new land policy.[7]

In 1929 the Commission submitted its report, recommending a new system for the disposal of crown lands, in which long-term leases should replace sales and the uses of entire land areas should be planned. Within any area, allotments should take place according to the following schedule of priorities: (1) land needs of the local village population, (2) land needs of villagers from other, congested areas, (3) conservation, (4) the neighborhood's need of forested land, (5) leases to "middle class" Ceylonese, (6) leases to other persons. These recommendations embodied in the 1929 report became principles of land policy adopted by semi-autonomous and free Ceylon.[8]

A much less significant development measure, enacted in the Legislative Council's dying days in response to insistent Ceylonese demands, was the establishment of a State Mortgage Bank with powers to lend on satisfactory real estate titles. Ceylonese spokes-

[5] *Report of the Committee on Utilization of Crown Lands* (Sessional Paper III, 1953), pp. 3, 7.
[6] *Ibid.*, pp. 3, 7, 9.
[7] *Ibid.*, pp. 7-9.
[8] *Ibid.*, pp. 8-9; International Bank Mission, *Economic Development of Ceylon*, p. 361.

men hoped that the bank would be a major stimulus to commercial, industrial, and agricultural growth and would enable the island's nationals to compete much more successfully with British enterprise.[9] Since the new agency extended only a modest volume of loans, legislators and others soon complained that it did not meet local needs for credit. But it is doubtful that a liberal lending policy would have brought about much agricultural expansion in those years. Markets were not favorable for agricultural investment.[10]   Tea and rubber were under acreage restriction.

When the semi-autonomous State Council became Ceylon's legislature in 1931, it, as well as private investors, chose to move cautiously. This was not chiefly ascribable to limited legislative powers. The Council selected a Board of Ministers from their own ranks, so that the Ceylonese were now able to initiate and develop most of the islands' economic policies. The colonial Governor retained the power of veto, plus responsibility for administration, foreign relations, and certain other matters; but the Governor preferred usually to co-operate with the Ceylonese lawmakers rather than to fight them by vetoing or imposing legislation.[11]   It was especially unlikely that he would block an agricultural development program, as long as the Council raised the necessary funds.

Finance was the major obstacle. Slim foreign balances, low export prices, and an unfavorable foreign loan market ruled out clearance, irrigation, and construction projects involving sizable imports of capital equipment. Ceylon's abundant labor could have been put to work, even without modern machinery, clearing and irrigating Dry Zone areas; but in the absence of machinery progress was bound to be slow, and payrolls as well as equipment purchases involved expense. Moreover, to induce large numbers of peasants to move from their villages into the malaria-ridden Dry Zone, monetary subsidies as well as grants of cleared land would have been necessary. The landless and very poor, who in a sense had the greatest inducement to move, were also those least able to support

---

[9] Leg., *1927*, p. 1209; *1930*, p. 1083; *1931*, pp. 602-3.

[10] *Report of the Committee on Utilization of Crown Lands*, p. 9; *Six-Year Programme of Investment*, pp. 270-71.

[11] I. D. S. Weerawardana, *Government and Politics in Ceylon, 1931-46*, pp. 29-65.

themselves during an interim period.[12] The State Council shrank from the outlays that ambitious land development would have required.[13]

But this does not mean that the first State Council adopted a do-nothing policy or did not subsidize Dry Zone colonization at all. After 1932 the government offered peasant settlers not only free, cleared land (on long-term lease), but also free timber, medical and veterinary assistance, advice, and three years' exemption from irrigation fees.[14] The Ministry of Agriculture and Lands calculated that it could safely plan to settle 2,500 acres during the initial stage of the program. In accordance with the Land Commission's recommendations, this new acreage was to go to peasants. The Ministry believed that withholding crown land from "capitalists" would probably retard agricultural development, but that the policy of reserving most land for peasants, and allocating some to "middle class" settlers was socially preferable.[15]

With the later 1930's came higher export prices, higher incomes, increased tax revenues, and a 100-million-rupees credit from the Colonial Development Fund. The State Council now allocated much larger sums for development projects and by the end of the decade was spending twice as much yearly on irrigation works as had its predecessor. The subsidies offered colonists remained the same, however, and the colonies attracted only a small number of peasant settlers. By 1939 the government had moved farmers on to less than 7,000 new acres in the Dry Zone.[16]

Other, less important features of the prewar agricultural development program included protection for a few minor crops and some state assistance to agricultural credit co-operatives. The protection came in part via tariffs, in part via a statute forcing importers to buy minimum percentages of various supplies from local sources.[17] The

[12] See Sir Ivor Jennings, *The Economy of Ceylon* (Madras: Oxford University Press, 1951), p. 63.
[13] The Executive Committee of Agriculture and Lands further argued that subsidized colonization had so far proved to be disappointing. (See *State, 1932*, pp. 333-42, 3111-15.)
[14] Jennings, *op. cit.*, p. 64.
[15] *State, 1932*, pp. 688-89, 3111-15.
[16] International Bank Mission, *op. cit.*, p. 422; *Economic and Social Development of Ceylon (A Survey), 1926-1954* (Colombo: Ceylon Government Press, July 1, 1955), p. 8.
[17] But this "Agricultural Products (Regulation) Act" dates only from 1939.

aid given through credit co-operatives was quite limited and probably had a greater redistributive than developmental effect. Peasant debtors paid very high rates to private money lenders.[18]

After 1938 "rural reconstruction" was an additional program attempting to raise living standards in village areas. Six years later the Acting Registrar of Co-operative Societies described the program thus:

Put in a nut-shell, the object of the entire scheme is to cure rural ills by making a direct and concerted attack on five fronts, namely, social, physical, mental, economic and spiritual. . . . The real value of the centres (set up under the program) is to be judged by the change they ultimately bring about in the psychology of the villagers. Their functions are in the last resort educational and they can be deemed to have achieved lasting results only if they have been able to make the villager industrious, self-reliant, and permanently improvement-minded. . . . The task of Rural Reconstruction is essentially organizational. Its object is the economic and social betterment of the rural inhabitants, and it is well known that the economic and social ills of the rural inhabitants are mainly due to a helplessness arising out of his incapacity to organize himself.

He also commented ruefully: ". . . Rural Reconstruction is getting to be considerably overdone in this country. The gospel has suffered through 'hot gospelling' and is in danger of developing into what is vulgarly called a 'racket.' "[19]

Meanwhile, the advent of war had forced Ceylon to pay more attention to immediate needs than to long-range development. As early as 1939 the government took steps to make the island more nearly self-sufficient in food; after the Japanese occupation of Burma cut off the rice imports that had normally fed about half the population, the threat of a food shortage was serious indeed. The government's chief concern was to increase food production with maximum speed. In order to put as much crown land as possible into cultivation, the Ministry of Agriculture and Lands offered short-term leases to whoever would agree to grow food crops; the schedule of priorities set up by the Land Commission was temporarily waived. The government also sought to achieve further utilization of pri-

[18] See Jennings, *The Economy of Ceylon*, pp. 53-54, 74-75.
[19] *Report on Rural Reconstruction in Ceylon* (Sessional Paper XXIII, 1944), pp. 9, 13, 29, 53.

vately owned lands by compelling tea and other plantations to raise food or contribute to a special food-production fund.[20]

But the wartime emphasis on rapidly increased output did not entirely rule out long-range development in accordance with prewar social policy. Rather, the government's anxiety to cultivate new lands caused it to offer much more generous terms to peasant settlers. After 1939 peasant colonists moving into the Dry Zone received not only the earlier benefits of cleared land, free timber, advice, medical assistance, and three years' remission of irrigation rates, but also a family dwelling place, a cash subsidy for stumping and further preparing the land, a few months' subsistence allowance, and the loan of buffaloes and implements. These loans became gifts if the colonist improved the land and gave a generally satisfactory performance. Furthermore, the government took steps to market the colonists' produce.[21]

These terms made it possible for almost penniless peasants to cultivate the new areas, and greatly reduced reluctance to move into the Dry Zone. During 1939-47 new settlement (exclusive of temporary leases) took place more than twice as rapidly as during the preceding decade. Even so, the amount of agricultural land added via colonization was a very small percentage of the total acreage cultivated in Ceylon, and these additions were secured at a high cost. By the end of 1947 the total number of Dry Zone allotments made was only 2,977, the total area covered only 21,251 acres, while the total cost was more than 29 million rupees, or Rs. 9,800 per allotment and Rs. 1,325 per acre.[22]

A second part of the long-range development program was "village expansion," wherein the government made crown land adjoining peasant villages available for cultivation and bore one-half of the peasant settler's improvement costs. During 1939-47 the government allotted over 100,000 acres of crown land in this way, also purchased about 11,000 acres of privately held land for distribution among villagers. But only about 1 per cent of the land added to the village areas was suitable for paddy, and a

[20] *Six-Year Programme of Investment*, p. 177; *Economic and Social Development of Ceylon*, p. 7.

[21] *Six Year Programme of Investment*, pp. 175-77; *Economic and Social Development of Ceylon*, p. 8.

[22] *Economic and Social Development of Ceylon*, p. 8; Jennings, *The Economy of Ceylon*, p. 65.

similarly low percentage applied to the 25,000 acres of crown land made available to "middle class" farmers during the war and immediate postwar years.[23]   Most of the newly added land did not give as high yields as the Ceylonese average.

Nor, for that matter, did the acreage additions check the steady drop in cultivated area per capita, which was only three-quarters as great in 1946 as in 1931.   Since commerce and industry did not absorb most of the growing population, farm dwellers became more and more densely crowded.[24]   Production data do not supply full information with respect to yields, but agricultural development obviously lagged far behind ambitions.[25]

The chief postwar policy changes were quantitative rather than qualitative; the government vastly increased expenditure on its colonization and village-expansion programs.[26]   It also achieved much greater success in finding settlers willing to try their luck in the Dry Zone colonies.   Partly because of a highly successful antimalarial campaign, which almost eliminated the disease from the island, partly because of increasing population pressure in the older farming areas, the terms which the Ministry of Lands offered peasants looked far more attractive than in earlier years.   Between 1947 and 1954 colonists took up more than 100,000 acres, including more than 60,000 acres of paddy land.[27]

But not even this much more rapid colonization (plus village expansion in the older areas) ended the decline in acreage cultivated per capita.[28]   Moreover, the newly developed land was very expensive; in 1952 the cost of settling a colonist on four to five acres of irrigated land plus three acres of nonirrigated land was reported to be between 12,000 and 14,000 rupees.[29]   Because of these high costs and the peasants' new eagerness to become colonists, the govern-

---

[23] *Six-Year Programme of Investment,* pp. 174-77; *Economic and Social Development of Ceylon,* p. 8.

[24] In 1950 an estimated 26 per cent of the families engaged in agriculture held no land at all, another 16 per cent held less than one-half acre, and still another 12 per cent held less than an acre. Paddy holdings were of course even smaller (I. D. S. and M. I. Weerawardana, *Ceylon and Her Citizens,* pp. 32, 36).

[25] See *Report of the Committee on Utilization of Crown Lands,* p. 7; *Economic and Social Development of Ceylon,* pp. 59-65.

[26] International Bank Mission, *op. cit.,* pp. 422-23.

[27] *Economic and Social Development of Ceylon,* p. 8.

[28] *Six-Year Programme of Investment,* p. 159.

[29] International Bank Mission, *op. cit.,* p. 425.

ment after 1952 reduced the 1939 schedule of settlers' benefits. During 1955-56 there was much talk that the benefits should be reduced yet further, as colonists still appeared to be a favored class among the poverty-stricken farmers of Ceylon.[30]

Crown land settled in the older cultivated areas, through village expansion schemes, totaled over 200,000 acres during 1947-54, at an average cost far below that of Dry Zone colonization. But since only a minute fraction of this was suitable for paddy, the acreage represented by village expansion was more impressive than the increased production.[31] During the first several postwar years the government swelled its village expansion program by purchasing a few thousand privately owned acres where little or no crown land was available, but it later became much more cautious, as land prices rose and experience showed that fragmentation of estates usually led to decreased production and wasted resources.[32] The government's chief hopes for increased output in the older food-growing areas were more intensive and more skilful farming, to be achieved via government advice and demonstration and the work of rural reconstruction and co-operative societies.[33]

As during the 1930's, little energy went into acreage expansion schemes other than those for the island's overcrowded and often landless peasants. During 1947-54 the government did, however, lease some 28,000 acres of crown land to "middle class" farmers, to whom it offered credit at low interest rates.[34] Little new acreage was put in plantation crops, but the state helped planters increase tea, rubber, and coconut yields per acre; among various aids extended was a rubber replanting subsidy inaugurated after Ceylon arranged to sell rubber to China at a price somewhat above the prevailing world level.[35] As in prewar years, import duties and other devices offered protection to farmers growing certain minor crops.

Perhaps a final word on agricultural policy under free Ceylon's first two Parliaments should concern Ceylonese planters' state-aided

[30] *Six-Year Programme of Investment*, pp. 180-81, 196-98.
[31] *Economic and Social Development of Ceylon*, p. 8; International Bank Mission, *op. cit.*, pp. 422-23
[32] *Six-Year Programme of Investment*, pp. 181-82.
[33] *Ibid.*, pp. 199-222.
[34] *Ibid.*, pp. 174, 182.
[35] *Economic and Social Development of Ceylon*, p. 8; *Six-Year Programme of Investment*, pp. 161-67.

purchases of British tea and rubber estates.[36]   Since these purchases decreased foreign claims upon the Ceylonese economy, they in a sense added to Ceylon's agricultural assets (at the cost of other assets which might have been acquired with the foreign exchange).   Some observers have claimed, however, that the transfer of ownership decreased productivity by putting easily destructible assets into the hands of investors accustomed to quick returns rather than cautious maintenance and improvement.   Foreign observers have also argued that the island's Ceylonization-of-employment program retards, rather than speeds, agricultural development.[37]

The first several months of the new Parliament as well as the election platform indicate that the People's United Front probably will not depart from the main outlines of its predecessor's agricultural policy: i.e., emphasis upon greater self-sufficiency, more land for peasants, and "rural reconstruction."   As Chapter II has stated, it is by no means sure that the new Cabinet will strive to please its more radically nationalist followers by nationalizing foreign estates or dividing them among villagers.   In June, 1956, the Minister of Agriculture and Food stated that the government would shortly take steps to end fragmentation of British estates purchased by Ceylonese.   Other announced policies would continue to help tea, rubber, and coconut planters increase per-acre yields.[38]

INDUSTRIAL DEVELOPMENT POLICY

Official interest in manufactures came later than that in commercial crops.   Before World War I the colonial government appears not to have asked what it could do to stimulate industry. Hundreds of factories did indeed spring up on the island, but nearly all these were part of the plantation economy; tea factories, rubber mills, and coconut oil mills processed the three export commodities so that they would be in a suitable condition to be shipped abroad.[39]

[36] Some purchasers secured the necessary funds from state-aided credit corporations.

[37] *House, 1949-50*, v. 7, c. 1964; International Bank Mission, *op. cit.*, pp. 225, 361-62; *Ceylon News*, June 28, 1956, p. 6 (statement by Minister of Agriculture and Food).

[38] See the *Ceylon News*, June 28, 1956, p. 6; also the issue of Aug. 30, 1956, which published a statement by the Minister of Lands and Land Development on achievements, problems, and plans for the future.

[39] Most Ceylonese do not regard tea and rubber factories, which are located on plantations, as "industrial" establishments.

In 1916 wartime shortages and perhaps other causes moved the Governor to appoint an Industries Commission to "inquire into and report upon what measures are desirable to encourage such industries (other than agricultural) as exist in this Island and to promote the establishment of new industries."[40] The Commission's *Report*, issued in 1922, argued that industrial development must wait upon the provision of cheap power, which in Ceylon's case could come only through a hydroelectric project. What the Commission termed its "most important" recommendation, however, was the establishment of a "Central Bureau of Industry and Research" to undertake research, give advice to private enterprise, and advertise Ceylon's products abroad.[41]

The colonial government acted upon the former of the two recommendations, appropriating funds for the 1924 commencement of work upon a "Hydro-Electric Scheme" intended to lay the foundation for the island's industrial future. But through some combination of bad planning, mismanagement, and ill luck, work on the project proved to be singularly ineffective; engineers' estimates and actual achievements differed by wide margins. By 1927 work had virtually stopped, and although in 1930 the Legislative Council indignantly rejected a proposal to sell the incomplete installations to a British corporation, the great depression so depleted Ceylon's treasury that work was not resumed until late in the decade.[42] World War II then intervened, and it was not until 1950 that the hydroelectric project supplied power. Even then the current went chiefly for household and mercantile use rather than to supply industrial power.[43]

The hydroelectric program was the government's most ambitious —if unsuccessful—development project before constitutional reform gave the Ceylonese a greater measure of self-government in 1931. The long-demanded State Mortgage Bank was voted into existence in the dying days of the old regime, and when it commenced operation, its limited powers and cautious loan policies plus the great depression

[40] *Report of the Industries Commission* (Sessional Paper I, 1922), pp. 3-4.
[41] *Ibid.*, pp. 8, 10.
[42] *Leg., 1929*, p. 1531; *Ceylon Hydro-Electric Scheme* (Sessional Paper XV, 1934), pp. 3-5.
[43] Prior to 1950 many Ceylonese towns and tea and rubber estates had their own small plants (International Bank Mission, *op. cit.*, pp. 455, 457, 473).

and investor timidity reduced its industrial significance to almost nil.[44]

Because of the great depression, the first State Council was even less ambitious than the colonial officials who initiated policy during the 1920's. In 1933 the Executive Committee of Labour, Industry and Commerce argued that the government's industrial functions should, in normal years, be to conduct research, construct and operate model factories, and grant loans to private enterprise; but that because of the treasury's weakness, the only feasible immediate function was research. Moreover, the Executive Committee opposed, as too expensive, the establishment of a research institute. A 1935 report shows that the industrial research undertaken during the State Council's first several years was meager indeed.[45]

The second State Council, elected in 1936, had more ambitious plans, thanks to higher export prices, higher incomes, increased tax revenues, and the 100-million-rupees loan from the Colonial Development Fund. Three million rupees were allocated for industrial ventures, and the Executive Committee of Labour, Industry and Commerce now thought it time to assume the duties earlier assigned for normal years. The Department of Commerce and Industries established to administer the industrial program sought to increase the supply of needed skills by sending Ceylonese abroad as trainees and students.[46]

With respect to the choice of industries, announced government policy was to serve local needs. The "needs" which were to be served, however, were not always consumer demands or even producer demands for materials and equipment to satisfy local consumption. Thus, a proposed plywood factory was intended to produce packing chests for the agricultural export industries, and some of the chemical industries which were under consideration also were intended to serve this general market. With respect to ownership and management, government policy was to rely primarily upon private enterprise and to aid that enterprise in various ways. State-owned model factories were not meant to be monopolies or even to compete with private business, but rather to show the way. The

[44] *Six-Year Programme of Investment*, pp. 270-71; International Bank Mission, *op. cit.*, p. 162.

[45] *State, 1933*, pp. 2234, 2933-35; *First Interim Report of the Technical Adviser on Industries* (Sessional Paper XV, 1953), p. 3.

[46] *Administrative Report of the Director of Commerce and Industries for the Year 1938*, pp. W28-W35.

State Council hoped that profit-seeking shareholders would shortly relieve the government of its entrepreneurial and managerial functions.[47]

To enable private enterprise to play its appointed role more effectively, the State Council helped it to acquire funds. To a certain extent this consisted of direct governmental loans.[48] The greatest hopes, however, were pinned to a state-aided bank, which had been proposed by the Ceylon Banking Commission in 1934 after experience with the State Mortgage Bank had turned out to be unsatisfactory. As the Commission and Council initially planned the bank it was to be a commercial, savings, and investment institution, all three, with the power to "underwrite, subscribe and invest in shares of joint-stock banks and other companies registered in Ceylon," buy and sell securities of the Ceylon government and foreign governments, and lend on the security of immovable properties, agricultural and manufacturing commodities, debentures, and other collateral. British colonial officials, however, strongly disapproved of a bank with such comprehensive powers and vetoed the initial bill. The statute finally approved in 1938 established a strictly commercial Bank of Ceylon which could not compete with the State Mortgage Bank by extending loans on real property and could not act as an investment banking institution.[49]

The government's principal industrial achievements during the late 1930's were the resumption of work on the hydro-electric project, the completion of various industrial surveys and special studies, and the construction of a coir factory (processing fiber from coconut husks). In 1937 the Minister of Labour, Industry and Commerce announced plans to start experimental textile factories as cottage industries, but in 1939 he reported that his Ministry had not been

[47] *State, 1939,* pp. 3107-3118; *1940,* pp. 1642, 1651-54.
[48] *Administrative Report of the Director of Commerce and Industries for the Year 1938,* pp. W29-W33.
[49] *State, 1935,* pp. 439, 669-83, 711-35, 830-39, 851; *1938,* pp. 282-85, 464 84; *Report of the Ceylon Banking Commission,* esp. pp. 84-85; G. C. S. Corea, "The State-Aided Bank," *Ceylon Economic Journal,* Dec., 1937.

When the Minister of Labor, Industry and Commerce asked the State Council to approve the new bill, he added that he would shortly propose an Agricultural and Industrial Credit Corporation to fill the gaps left by the Bank of Ceylon and the State Mortgage Bank. This additional corporation was voted into existence in 1940, but its record shows little aid to industrial development (International Bank Mission, *op. cit.,* pp. 517-18).

able to work out all the necessary details. Late in 1939 the State Council appropriated funds for a plywood factory which commenced operations in 1942. Other industrial projects were still in the planning stage when war broke out in Europe.[50]

Since the war diverted shipping and Western industrial capacity from normal peacetime uses, consumer and other imports soon were not available in demanded quantities. There was thus a much more favorable market for Ceylonese manufactures than in earlier years; among the goods in short supply were not only those which the Department of Commerce and Industries had earlier planned to produce, but also some which the Department had thought should continue to be imported. Most of the wartime factories, however, including plywood, acetic acid, drugs, steel, ceramics, glass, and leather, had been in the prewar scheduled list. Only the hat and paper factories represented departures from the planned program.[51]

In 1946 the Executive Committee of Labour, Industry and Commerce explained their wartime choice of new factories thus:

. . . we were of the opinion that it should not be the policy of Government to embark on a course of the action which might savour of indiscriminate industrial development to meet ad hoc needs as and when they arose, especially when the period of duration of the emergency was unpredictable. In selecting the industries to be developed we adopted the policy of selecting those which on expert advice and from the point of view of availability of natural resources we were assured that permanency in establishment was quite within the realms of realisation.[52]

Unfortunately, the same wartime conditions that handicapped customary trade put new obstacles in the way of a development program. Busy with the job of supplying their fighting forces, the Commonwealth countries and America did not wish to divert resources to producing capital equipment or providing technicians and training programs for Ceylon. The Ministry of Labour, Industries and Commerce thus had to substitute freely for machinery and skills specified in prewar plans. In 1953 an investigating commission applauded the Ministry for "its romantic resourcefulness in conjuring

[50] Report on Industrial Development and Policy, p. 6; Administrative Report of the Director of Commerce and Industries for the Year 1938, . . . for the Year 1939.
[51] Report on Industrial Development and Policy, p. 6; Administration Report of the Acting Director of Industries for the Years 1940 to 1947, pp. GG8-18.
[52] Report on Industrial Development and Policy, p. 9.

up an Acetic Acid Factory, a Steel Rolling Factory, a Drugs Factory or a Paper Mill out of practically nothing in order to provide for the starving needs of a country during a period of direst difficulty."[53] During the war years most of the government factories reported a net profit, since inflated Ceylonese incomes and lack of foreign competition offset improvised production methods plus weaknesses in management and labor skills. Their postwar record became increasingly unsatisfactory, however, and by 1955 most had been closed.[54] The Ministry did not achieve the "permanency of establishment" intended.

A second part of the wartime industrial program was progress in cottage industries, approximately in accordance with prewar plans. By 1946 the Ministry of Labour, Industry and Commerce was able to report that it had established 449 "centres," 88 "workshops," and 166 training schools. Most of these produced textiles, but coir, pottery, mats, and carpentry also received much attention. On the average, these fared better than the factories, although many did not long survive.[55]

The new cottage industries involved varying combinations of governmental control and private enterprise. The factories were state-owned and operated and, by the end of the war, were intended to remain that way. This was one respect in which the State Council's industrial policy changed substantially during the war. As late as 1940 the Executive Committee of Labour, Industry and Commerce hoped to rely primarily upon private enterprise,[56] but their repeated failure to interest private capital in industries which the government wished to develop finally led them to look upon state ownership and management as the normal and preferable means of progress in at least the "basic" industries, which were defined very broadly indeed. "In the nature of the existing economic development of this country," stated the Executive Committee of Labour, Industry

[53] *Report of the Commission on Government Commercial Undertakings*, pp. 2-3. For a more detailed account, see *Administration Report of the Acting Director of Industries for the Years 1940 to 1947*, pp. GG8-9.

[54] *Report of the Commission on Government Commercial Undertakings*, pp. 34-43, 53-57, 83-87; *Six-Year Programme of Investment*, pp. 235-36.

[55] *Report on Industrial Development and Policy*, pp. 11-12; *Report of the Commission on Government Commercial Undertakings*, pp. 43, 53-54.

[56] *State*, 1940, pp. 1642, 1651-54.

and Commerce, "we consider the following industries should be regarded as falling under the group of basic industries:

(1) Power.

(2) Heavy Industries—viz., Iron, Steel and Cement.

(3) Heavy Chemicals, including the group of fertilizer chemicals.

(4) Specified Drugs and Pharmaceuticals.

(5) Cotton Spinning."[57]

"We have given careful thought," continued the Executive Committee,

to the question of how basic industries could be developed with advantage to the national economy. It is our considered recommendation that they should be nationalised and be the exclusive monopoly of State enterprise . . . . We . . . recommend with respect to non-basic industries that private enterprise should be permitted to undertake and develop such industries as they may desire to do. . . . If private enterprise is not responsive, then it should be left to the Minister in charge of Industries . . . [to] decide whether such an industry even though not on the basic list should be established by the Government alone or in some form of partnership with private enterprise.

The government should conduct research and encourage private in-investment in such fields.[58]

The Executive Committee was less friendly to foreign firms. Before allowing foreign entry, they recommended, the government should

satisfy itself inter alia that (1) the establishment of such an industrial enterprise will not be prejudicial to local industries already established or with possibilities of economic local development, (2) at least a prescribed percentage of the share-capital is offered for local subscription, and (3) at least a certain percentage of employment is offered to indigenous labor.[59]

A year after the Executive Committee submitted its report, Parliament replaced the State Council and Ceylon enjoyed the full independence that was formally recognized early in 1948. The United National Party, which essentially represented the groups dominant in State Council days, was elected to power and dominated

[57] *Report on Industrial Development and Policy*, pp. 8, 15-20 (quoted passage from p. 17).

[58] *Ibid.*, pp. 18, 20.

[59] *Ibid.*, p. 23.

the first two Parliaments (1947-52, 1952-56) of free Ceylon. Industrial policy under the United National party went through three phases, those of 1947-50, 1951-53, and 1954-56. During the first period government policy was little different from that of the wartime and postwar State Council; during the second the initial policy was questioned; during the third the Cabinet went far towards adopting the program recommended by the International Bank Mission, with its emphasis on private enterprise, and thus retreated in large measure towards the policies announced during the prewar period.

During 1947-50 the government continued to operate most of the wartime factories and, although the sums allocated for manufacturing were much smaller than those budgeted for agriculture, the announced program included several new factories. The government also continued to reserve "basic industries" for government enterprise and to define "basic" rather broadly. Although the Cabinet welcomed "nonbasic" development via private enterprise, it did little to give private investors aid or encouragement.

Neither within the private nor the governmental sphere did much industrial progress take place. By 1952, when the International Bank Mission submitted its report, the only postwar factory which the government had completed was the cement plant initially scheduled much earlier and begun in 1946. The status of other government industrial projects was as follows: new paper factory—under construction; caustic soda plant—initial contracts let; textile factories, coconut oil mill, and new steel mill—still in the planning stage.[60] The Cabinet later stated that the delay was attributable in part to such causes as shortages of qualified technicians and slow deliveries from foreign suppliers, but also in part to needed revisions in engineering and related plans. A former Director of Commerce and Industries blamed the delay on administrative lacks.[61]

State factories already in operation also compiled a very bad record. By 1951 most had experienced such large losses that the Cabinet appointed an investigating commission, and by the following year most had been closed.[62] The Cabinet did not share some econ-

[60] International Bank Mission, op. cit., pp. 531 ff.
[61] Economic and Social Development of Ceylon, p. 48; Report of the Commission on Government Commercial Undertakings, p. 84.
[62] Op. cit., pp. 34-43, 53-57, 83-87.

omists' belief that even unprofitable factories were social assets if
they provided enough employment;[63] in 1949 the Minister of Industries explicitly stated, "This (government-owned factory) is not
an unemployment relief scheme."[64]   As with respect to the new
factories' slow progress, so with respect to the old factories' losses,
there was much controversy as to the cause. The former civil servant
mentioned above argued that the improvised wartime factories were
not expected to last beyond 1947; in 1953 the investigating commission placed much blame on bad planning and the red tape involved in direct governmental management, and recommended that
the factories be converted into semi-independent public corporations.[65]

Meanwhile the International Bank Mission had submitted its
report, criticizing certain industrial projects already commenced or under study, and deploring the Cabinet's emphasis upon state enterprise
and failure to aid and encourage private entrepreneurs. The Mission
advised that the government should act as a pioneer, but that industrial progress would be swifter and production greater if established
concerns were sold to private shareholders. The Mission also proposed the establishment of certain development agencies, including
a research institute and a development corporation to aid both
government and private enterprise, and urged that Ceylon more
actively seek the capital and skills which foreign private enterprise
could bring.[66]

In 1954 the Minister of Industries announced a revised industrial
policy largely corresponding to that which the Mission recommended.
Nine policy features believed to be "both necessary and sufficient for
immediate study and application" were:

(1) promotion of small-scale enterprises; (2) encouragement of foreign
capital and in large-scale undertakings; (3) assistance to local industry—
both large and small; (4) directional control of capital movement in Ceylon; (5) participation of Government in private enterprise; (6) re-drafting
of industrial legislation; (7) acceleration of industrial research; (8) co-
ordination and systemization of training facilities; and (9) standardization
of industrial products.[67]

[63] E. g., C. Suriyakumaran, *Ceylon, Beveridge and Bretton Woods*, pp. 37-42.
[64] *House, 1949-50*, v. 6, c. 2330.
[65] *Report of the Commission on Government Commercial Undertakings*, pp.
19-23, 63-68, 84-88.
[66] International Bank Mission, *op. cit.*, pp. 120-21, 126, 505-606.
[67] *Senate, 1954-55*, v. 8, c. 661-86 (quoted passage from c. 677).

The following year the Cabinet spelled out further details of its new industrial policy.[68]   Of the 112 million rupees allocated to industry under the Six-Year Programme, Rs. 43.3 million were scheduled for existing state enterprises (in operation or under construction), Rs. 26 million for government participation in "large-scale" industry (20 per cent of these enterprises' total capital), Rs. 9.8 million for assistance to small-scale industry (again 20 per cent of the total capital), Rs. 24.3 million to cottage industries, and Rs. 8.4 million for industrial research and training.   As the Planning Secretariat pointed out, this distribution represented a lesser degree of emphasis on "large-scale" industries than in the past, a greater degree of emphasis upon small-scale and cottage industries.

Greater reliance on private enterprise was to be sought through the features of a government-sponsored-corporations act, enabling transfer of factories from government to private ownership in three stages: first, the transfer from a government department to a semi-independent public corporation; next, the sale of shares to private investors; and finally, the withdrawal of government from the picture. To help provide funds and skills for new industrial ventures, the government established the Ceylon Development Corporation which the International Bank Mission had recommended.   Other development agencies established under the new policy were a semigovernmental Institute of Scientific and Industrial Research, a Planning Secretariat, and a Development Advisory Board; the last two had other as well as industrial responsibilities.

In the spring of 1956, when the U. N. P. was voted out of power, the roster of government factories (still under departmental management or transferred to semi-independent corporations) included cement, plywood, leather, ceramics, paper, vegetable oil, and caustic soda-chlorine.   The last three, however, were not yet in operation, and a Japanese industrial mission asked to report on the government factories found much fault with engineering and other features of both completed and unfinished plants.[69]   The Department of Industries hoped that construction could begin before long on several other factories then in the planning stage,[70] and tried to interest both

[68] *Six-Year Programme of Investment*, pp. 28, 35, 61-64, 234-73.

[69] *Ceylon Daily News*, Aug. 19, 1955, "Economic Supplement."

[70] Government-sponsored factories in the planning stage were kaolin, asbestos cement, barbed wire and rolled steel, glassware, dry cells, confectionery and sugar.

Ceylonese and foreign private enterprise in still other manufacturing ventures. Within the area of cottage industry, the principal announced program was the establishment of new weaving centers, including power-loom as well as hand-loom projects.[71]

Tariff and other protection played a major role in Parliament's industrial plans. ". . . I will not permit my country to become the dumping ground of damaged goods of other countries," cried the Finance Minister in December, 1947. The Ceylonese government, he declared, had a "duty . . . to see that our people are not made to buy cheap goods from markets of the more advanced countries of the world."[72] Protectionist measures employed included tariffs, exchange controls, quotas, and the Industrial Products Act, which forced importers of administratively specified commodities to purchase certain percentages of their supplies from local producers.[73]

Ceylonese policy-makers and other spokesmen apparently regarded protection against foreign firms as another necessary development measure. In general, Cabinet policy before 1954 followed the lines recommended by the Executive Committee's 1946 *Report:* i.e., it did not entirely forbid foreign firms' entry, but prevented competition with existing or potential Ceylonese firms and allowed no entry except when the foreign firm would accept Ceylonese partners and trainees.[74] During 1954-56 the Cabinet did not radically alter terms offered foreign firms, but, since they no longer reserved "basic" industries as state monopolies, they opened potential new areas for all private investors and encouraged Ceylonese businessmen to associate with foreign firms in order to gain both capital and "know-how."[75] Moreover, the tax laws embodied various "incentive" features to attract private and foreign capital alike.[76]

[71] In February, 1956, a second Japanese mission arrived to study potential new cottage and small-factory industries. For the list of mentioned possibilities, see *Ceylon Daily News*, Feb. 15, 1956.

[72] *House, 1947-48*, v. 1, c. 1440.

[73] One reason for this last form of protection was Ceylon's signature to the General Agreement on Trade and Tariffs, which forbade other new unilateral protectionist moves. See the debate in *House, 1948-49*, v. 5, c. 1676-91, 1711.

[74] One exception here was Bata's entry as a manufacturer of canvas-and-rubber shoes. See below, chap. vi, n. 15. For Cabinet speeches on foreign enterprise, see *House, 1948-49*, v. 3, c. 1045-46; v. 4, c. 1321-22; *1949-50*, v. 6, c. 128-130; *1950-51*, v. 8, c. 178; *1951-52*, v. 11, c. 1602.

[75] See *Government Policy in Respect of Private Foreign Investment in Ceylon* (Colombo: Government Publications Bureau, July, 1955).

[76] See *Report of the Taxation Commission*, pp. 223-29.

Besides tariffs and tax concessions, government aid promised industrial investors included research assistance, technical advice and loans. The Cabinet's announced policy included these helps even during the years when "basic" industries were reserved for the state. Loans were to come from the Agricultural and Industrial Corporation and the state-aided but largely independent Bank of Ceylon. When the International Bank Mission studied the economy, however, they found little evidence of either technical or long-term financial aid.[77] The research institute and development corporation established in 1955 were intended to fill these lacks. Some seven months after the research institute commenced operations, the director reported that substantial progress was being made.[78] The development corporation had barely been organized before the 1956 election swept the United National party from power and installed a new Cabinet less friendly to private enterprise.

During its first several months, the new regime in some respects continued its predecessor's recent policies; that is, it proceeded with work on partially begun and planned factories, it employed semi-independent corporations rather than government departments as administering organizations,[79] and it sought to secure some union of private and foreign capital for the development of certain industries which the government did not itself intend to enter. But in other major respects the industrial policy of the People's United Front appears to reverse the pre-1956 trend; emphasis has been shifted back from cottage to factory industries; and, although the Cabinet has announced that it will offer new tax concessions to private investors, "basic" industries appear once again to be reserved for the state. Moreover, the "partnership" terms which the present Cabinet offers to foreign enterprise are probably less favorable than those which the United National party came to believe necessary after 1953.[80] Little private foreign capital entered Ceylon under the U. N. P.; less is likely to under the new regime.

[77] International Bank Mission, op. cit., pp. 514-21, 795-97.

[78] Ceylon Daily News, Nov. 25, 1955, "Economic Supplement."

[79] Factories planned and under construction, as reported in the Ceylon News, include cement, textiles, salt, acetic acid, fertilizer, and kaolin. The National Kaolin Corporation was established in October, 1956. The textile factory apparently replaces cottage-industry textile "centres" included in the U. N. P. Six-Year Programme.

[80] The People's United Front declared in its election platform: "All key industries must be run by the State. Small industries such as cottage industries

DEVELOPMENT FINANCE: PRIVATE AND GOVERNMENTAL

All governments of Ceylon have expected private enterprise to finance at least part of the hoped-for development. The colonial regime expected much of the initiative and capital to come from British sources, and up through the prosperous mid-1920's much of the private finance that developed the island came from the imperial country. British proprietors and shareholders supplied equity capital for the development of export agriculture and related trades and services; British branch banks and other financial institutions advanced funds to private enterprise on short-term and long-term loan.[81] The prewar State Council placed chief reliance upon Ceylonese investors, and hoped that the State Mortgage Bank and state-aided Bank of Ceylon would enable Ceylonese capitalists simultaneously to increase the nation's wealth and to compete with British enterprise for financial supremacy on the island. The wartime State Council and first Parliament relied much less on private enterprise, but hoped that, with aid from the banks and the Agricultural and Industrial Credit Corporation, Ceylonese capitalists would shoulder an appreciable part of the development burden. The post-1953 Cabinet moved back towards a greater emphasis on private finance, heavily assisted by the Ceylon Development Corporation.

During much of the period, taxes were favorable for Ceylonese capital formation. The inheritance tax imposed in 1919 was light;[82] income was not taxed until 1932, and then only at a low rate;[83] export duties cut heavily into tea planters' incomes, but in good years these were high in spite of the duties and they were mostly British rather than Ceylonese. Income tax rates were raised during the forties and fifties, so that they finally became very high;[84] but the

---

can be in the hands of private enterprise" (*Free Lanka,* March 11, 1956, p. 3). Stories on postelection policy with respect to cottage and factory industries, state and private enterprise, government corporations, and foreign investment appear in the *Ceylon News,* July 19, 1956, p. 16; Aug. 2, 1956, p. 8; Jan. 10, 1957, p. 3.

[81] For a Ceylonese view on the functions of British financial institutions, see *Report of the Banking Commission,* pp. 9, 25-30, 71.

[82] Marginal tax rates were from 1 to 3 per cent, the basic exemption Rs. 1500. In 1926 the exemption was raised to Rs. 5,000. After 1947 marginal rates were 3-40 per cent, the basic exemption Rs. 20,000 (*Report of the Taxation Commission,* p. 254).

[83] Basic exemption was Rs. 2,000; marginal rates on higher incomes were 5, 10, and 15 per cent. By 1940 the marginal rates were 7.5, 15, 22.5 per cent (*ibid.,* pp. 211-12).

[84] Basic exemption in 1955 was still Rs. 2,000, although prices were several

government in part offset the high rates by offering special concessions to persons and corporations undertaking approved types of investment.[85] Taxes are not so high as to keep Ceylonese private investment from rising above its current level.

Ceylonese consumption habits may, however, keep savings from substantially rising. The island's population does not in large measure share those attitudes towards pleasure, leisure, and acquisition which some historians trace to "the Protestant ethic" and believe responsible for rapid capital formation in the West.[86] According to some observers, "conspicuous consumption" keeps upper-income families' saving from reaching desirably high levels;[87] the bulk of the Ceylonese receive such low incomes that only heroic abstinence makes appreciable saving possible. To some extent upper-income families' small savings may also be attributable to what various observers have called "lack of enterprise," which prevents entrepreneurial use of savings and thus reduces the incentive to save. But many of those who talk about "lack of enterprise" chiefly have in mind the unproductive uses of funds actually saved: e.g., the speculative bidding up of prices of already developed properties.[88]

Private *gross* investment is thought to have been about 5 per cent of gross national product in 1938 and to have varied around that percentage during 1947-53, reaching a high of 7 per cent during the Korean War boom.[89] Appearances indicate that private investment was probably a little above its average level in 1955, as various small-scale ventures got under way.

Like other governments, the government of Ceylon has financed expenditures out of both taxes and borrowed funds. Before 1932 export, import, and excise duties provided the bulk of the revenues; after that the income tax also was an important part of the picture,

times higher than in 1932. Marginal rates ranged from 10 per cent on the first taxable Rs. 6,000 to 85 per cent on taxable income above Rs. 120,000 (*ibid.*, p. 214). The exchange value of a rupee is roughly $0.21, but the cost of living in Ceylon is much lower than in the United States.

[85] *Ibid.*, pp. 223-28.

[86] A visitor with pleasant memories of a people who enjoy pleasure and leisure can only hope that adequate capital formation will not require the "Protestant" attitudes.

[87] Jennings, *The Economy of Ceylon*, pp. 36-37; B. B. Das Gupta, "National Saving and Economic Development," *Ceylon Economist*, I (Aug., 1950), 9.

[88] Jennings, *op. cit.*, pp. 33-34.

[89] *Report of the Taxation Commission*, p. 71.

although indirect taxes continued in most years to provide two-thirds or more of the total sum collected.[90] During the period of British rule government securities were in large part sold to British investors; in 1937 the State Council secured a drawing account upon the Colonial Development Fund established in London for such purposes. After 1949, when Parliament established the Central Bank of Ceylon and gave it the power to create money, the Central Bank helped to take care of the government's credit needs. But, in order to gain foreign exchange, Ceylon sold securities in London and borrowed from the International Bank.

In general the logic of "loan fund expenditure" before the establishment of the Central Bank was that of traditional "orthodox" public finance. Borrowing was approved when its purpose was to add a long-range capital asset and when the funds were raised in such a way as not to create inflationary pressures in Ceylon.[91] For a short period after the Central Bank commenced operations, the Finance Minister appealed to "Keynesian" economics to defend budgetary deficits covered by new money; the deficit spending was intended simultaneously to increase employment and promote growth. But after the 1953 foreign-exchange crisis Cabinet speeches in effect admitted that Keynesian teachings applicable to closed economies did not apply to Ceylon.[92]

In spite of the hydroelectric project, or, perhaps, because of the project's ill fortune, "loan fund expenditure" during the nineteen twenties and early thirties remained a small fraction (usually less than 5 per cent) of total government outlay. Nor did it rise sharply immediately after the loan was secured from the Colonial Development Fund. As the following table shows, heavy spending out of borrowed funds first came with the wartime agricultural and industrial programs and continued with the development projects of postwar years.

In 1938 government *gross* investment was less than 1 per cent, and in 1947 it was only a little more then 1 per cent, of estimated

---

[90] *Economic and Social Development of Ceylon*, pp. 111-13

[91] See, *inter alia*, State, *1936*, pp. 3265-67.

[92] See *House*, *1949-50*, v. 6, c. 131-32, 136; v. 7, c. 723; *1952-53*, v. 12, c. 652; *1953-54*, v. 14, c. 234-35, 770-73; *1954-55*, v. 18, c. 4-15; also H. A. de S. Gunasekera, "Thoughts on Full Employment," *Ceylon Economist*, I (Nov., 1950), 191-98.

	TOTAL EXPENDITURE*	LOAN FUND EXPENDITURE*
1926-30.	619.3	22.1
1930-35.	490.6	12.4
1935-40.	583.1	24.3
1940-45.	931.7	114.5
1945-50.	2451.4	416.5
1950-55.	4361.8	992.3

* Millions of rupees

gross national product.   Thereafter the percentage rose from 2.5 in 1948 to 4.8 in 1951 to 7.0 in 1953.[93]

Ceylon basically has met the foreign-exchange requirements of its development programs by an excess of exports over consumer imports and payments on foreign investments in Ceylon.[94]   In recent years, however, it has received technical assistance and other benefits through the Colombo Plan, valued at about 20 million rupees per annum.[95]   In 1956 the United States made available an additional $5 million in technical assistance.   The foreign loans mentioned above have supplied temporary advances, increasing the size of export balances later required.   The 1937 credit obtained from the Colonial Development Corporation amounted to Rs. 100 million; the 1954 sale of securities in the London market, to £5 million; the International Bank loan to $19 million.[96]

During World War II Ceylon acquired, thanks to Britain's method of financing its war effort in south Asia, some Rs. 1,260 million in blocked sterling balances, which were gradually released during the postwar period.[97]   Much of this sterling appears to have been paid out for subsidized rice imports and Ceylonese purchases of British tea and rubber estates.   British contributions under the Colombo Plan have also in part been subtracted from Ceylonese sterling balances, rather than paid out of new grants voted by the House of Commons.

[93] *Report of the Taxation Commission,* p. 71.
[94] For trade statistics, see *Economic and Social Development of Ceylon,* pp. 66-82.
[95] *Six-Year Programme of Investment,* p. 54.
[96] The International Bank loan was used to cover foreign-exchange costs of Stage IIA of the hydroelectric project begun in the 1920's.   In late 1956 Ceylon asked the International Bank for an additional $18 million to cover foreign-exchange costs of Stage IIB (*Ceylon News,* Dec. 27, 1956, p. 2).
[97] International Bank Mission, *op. cit.,* pp. 144-147; *Economic and Social Development of Ceylon,* pp. 9-11, 67-71.

5

Economic Development:

II. Ceylonese Development Theory

EXPOSITIONS OF PRE-1940 THEORY

DURING the period when colonial officials manned the island's executive posts the Industries Commission's 1922 *Report* was the closest approach to a statement of official development theory, and the theory which it expounded was fragmentary.[1] The Commission's explicit reasoning was most nearly complete with respect to natural resources and the allocation of funds among alternative investments. "By reason of natural resources Ceylon is destined to be primarily an agricultural country. . . . Ceylon is not blessed with mineral wealth, and is absolutely deficient in coal and oil." Only a few new industries appeared to be "really capable of development on a sufficiently large scale to merit comparison as regards ultimate financial success with the old established industries. . . ." The return from investment in tea, rubber and coconuts, "and even in mortgages," the *Report* continued, was so great that any new industry would have to "show possibilities of at least an equal rate of return in order to attract capital."[2]

Ceylon's sole industrial hope, the Commission believed, lay in the harnessing of unutilized water power.

So far as we can judge, there is hardly a single manufacturing industry which, if developed on a large scale, under existing conditions, could ever give promise of reasonable success. If, however, the hydro-electric scheme were to materialize, Ceylon would be provided with a cheap

[1] Discussion preceding, and complementary to, the *Report of the Industries Commission* may be found in *Papers Relating to the Development of the Economic Resources of the Colony* (Sessional Paper VI, 1921).
[2] *Report of the Industries Commission*, pp. 7-10.

and efficient mechanical power, which would place the development of the Island's industries on an entirely different footing.[3]

For the vexing problems of managerial and labor skills, the *Report* suggested remedies in the form of government research and the teaching of suitable courses at the newly established Ceylon University College.[4]   Since Ceylon was then a colony expected long to remain a part of the Empire, the Commission may have believed that managerial shortages would also be remedied by imports from Britain.   With respect to enterprise and finance, about all that the *Report* explicitly stated is that the government should pioneer in the hydroelectric project.   But the Commission's reliance upon private enterprise in manufacturing proper is quite clear, and their implicit belief concerning finance seems to have been that private enterprise would provide the necessary savings and loan funds in about the same ways that it had in the prior development of the island: i.e., finances would come in part from British shareholders and banks and in part through the further growth of a Ceylonese capitalistic and entrepreneurial class, such as had pioneered and prospered in coconuts, plumbago (graphite), and certain lines of retail trade.[5]

The nature of the development theory which Ceylonese leaders expounded during the 1920's is best seen in their numerous, optimistic references to Japan.   Perhaps the most nearly complete exposition of this theory is found in editorials and special articles in the *Ceylon Economist*,[6] but the same general reasoning is explicit or implicit in other writings and in numerous speeches delivered in the Legislative Council.[7]   Much stress was placed on the role of the state, and especially on the government's obligation to provide would-be Ceylonese investors with the necessary funds, the lack of which was believed to be the chief obstacle to the island's commercial, industrial, and agricultural development and to Ceylonese competition with British enterprise.   Other government services which legislators often demanded were industrial research, training of management

[3] *Ibid., loc. cit.*
[4] *Ibid.*, pp. 7, 9, 19; *Papers Relating to the Development. . .* , p. 23.
[5] *Report of the Industries Commission*, pp. 7-8, 11, 19; *Papers Relating to the Development . . .* , pp. 44-45, 51.
[6] *Ceylon Economist*, April, 1919, pp. 66-67; May, 1919, p. 79; June, 1919, pp. 97-104; Nov., 1919, pp. 217-27.
[7] See especially *Leg., 1925*, pp. 326-27; *1926*, pp. 845-48.

and labor, and the protection of "infant and nascent industries" against foreign competition.

Ceylonese development theory received a more careful and more nearly complete statement in 1934, when the Ceylon Banking Commission issued its *Report*. The *Report's* emphasis was upon industrial growth, and among the questions which it discussed were the desirability of such growth, the reasons for its slow pace in Ceylon, the ways in which the government could push industrialization, banking reform as an industrial prerequisite, and the proper industrial roles of banks. "The most urgent problem," reported the Banking Commission, "is the opening up of new industries, both agricultural and manufacturing, with the main object of catering primarily for the home market and thereby rendering the economy less susceptible to the vagaries of markets abroad." Industrial development, it continued, had been impeded by lack of basic minerals and cheap electric power, also by the profits which investors could until recently gain from agricultural exports. But the slow pace of Ceylonese entry into trade and industry was attributable in part to the glamour surrounding government employment and the professions, to lack of confidence itself explained by lack of experience, and to British discrimination against Ceylonese would-be trainees and investors.[8]

In order to speed industrial development, the Banking Commission concluded, the government should push through the hydroelectric project to completion, undertake research, give technical advice, erect model factories, confer industrial scholarships, and advance needed funds, especially through a state-aided bank. A truly Ceylonese bank, the Commission argued, was a requisite of adequate economic development.

Unless there is behind the working of the banking system that patriotism and national enthusiasm which have stimulated and sustained the trade and industries of other countries, no nation can rise to its fullest economic stature. That is proved by the history of other nations. . . . The German credit system before the Great War transformed the nation, so to speak, overnight from an agricultural to an industrial country. . . . Japan's present industrial growth owes a great deal to her banking facilities.[9]

[8] *Report of the Banking Commission*, pp. 18-21.
[9] *Ibid.*, pp. 9, 28, 67-69, 180-88.

Other elements of a development theory were expounded by K. D. Guha, earlier of the Bengal Department of Industries, who served as Ceylon's Technical Adviser on Industries during 1934-39. Guha favored "a planned program of industrial activities," but, as he saw the future, the choice of planned programs was not wide. "The growth of industries and traditions is organic in nature and every country must pass through the normal phases," which are marked by "primitive agricultural production," "improved agricultural production," "small industries—improved cottage industries production," and "factory production."[10]

Ceylon, Guha argued, should initially stress the development of cottage industries: "The Socio-economic conditions of Ceylon which is more or less purely an agricultural country render it best suited to the improvement of cottage industry as a subsidiary occupation of the people, especially the cultivators." "In Ceylon as in India . . . the vast majority of the agricultural population hardly find any opportunity of employing their time and energy in any useful and productive occupation other than cultivation which in the absence of large holdings *per capita* and satisfactory irrigation facilities, does not give them enough employment all the year round." Similarly, Ceylonese temperament was better suited to cottage and other small-scale enterprise than to large factories, which "imply ruthless regimentation and separation from home." Moreover, Ceylon lacked an "industrial tradition" and a spirit of business enterprise, and the question of consumer purchasing power had to be considered. ". . . the success of the bigger industries will ultimately depend on the increased purchasing capacity of the villagers who are capable of being trained as cottage workers."[11]

The Technical Adviser also argued that, if Ceylonese factories were to succeed, the government would have to protect infant enterprise against both foreign and domestic competition. "Country-made articles competing with foreign imports are always looked upon with suspicion, and generally have to be sold at a much lower price to command the market, even when the quality is equally good." And if a local factory does achieve success,

[10] *First Interim Report of the Technical Adviser on Industries* (Sessional Paper XV, 1935), p. 20; K. D. Guha, "Certain Aspects of Industrial Planning in Ceylon," *Ceylon Economic Journal*, Dec., 1937, pp. 57-61.
[11] *First Interim Report . . .* , pp. 6, 19; K. D. Guha, *op. cit.*, pp. 59-60, 63.

rival enterprises are immediately started, the trained labour is enticed away, the cost of the material is sometimes enhanced, and competition, possibly in a weak market, has to be faced, with the result that the monopoly upon which a new venture must count to recoup extraordinary initial expenditure rapidly vanishes and profits are reduced to a level at which only those can work successfully who are benefited by the work of the pioneer without having to pay for that.[12]

Apart from Guha's, few if any writings during this period explicitly stressed the special problem posed by Ceylon's small market and asked specifically how this difficulty might be overcome. But much debate over the proposed licensing of new industrial enterprises reflected concern over factories' being able to realize economies of scale, and the government's choice of various industries (such as plywood manufacturing) apparently involved such considerations.[13] Guha's reasoning may not have been the determining influence, but the Executive Committee of Labour, Industry and Commerce later advanced arguments that sounded much like Guha's concerning the purchasing-power role of cottage industries and the need to protect industrial pioneers.[14]

Discussion of agricultural, as distinct from industrial, development was often coupled with proposals for economic reform. The leading agricultural expansion planned during the 1930's was the colonization of the Dry Zone; and, as has been pointed out, the Executive Committee of Agriculture and Lands favored a policy which they thought would retard development but offer greater opportunities to the landless and overcrowded. Once the choice was made for peasant rather than "capitalistic" expansion, the questions that arose concerned the means and costs of inducing peasant movement into the Dry Zone and successful cultivation thereafter. Debate chiefly arose with respect to the extent and nature of the subsidies to be offered and the measures to aid marketing of produce.[15]

[12] *First Interim Report* . . . , p. 18.

[13] *State, 1938,* p. 3833; *1940,* pp. 194-95, 407. The State Council voted against licensing except in the match industry, where a licensing-plus-quota system was established in 1937.

[14] *Report on Industrial Development and Policy,* pp. 12-22.

[15] See, *inter alia, State 1932,* pp. 333-40, 688-91, 2295-2303, 3111-15; D. S. Senanayake, "In Defence of Our Land and Agricultural Policy," *Ceylon Economic Journal,* VII (Dec., 1935), 3-6; C. V. Brayne, "The Problem of Peasant Agriculture in Ceylon," *Ceylon Economic Journal,* VI (Dec., 1934), 34-46.

Discussion of urgent problems of the older peasant areas perhaps showed even more clearly the relationship between development and reform.   Much writing and legislative debate concerned peasants' needs for cheap credit, to be provided via co-operative or special banks; and one of the questions which especially concerned economists and policy-makers was how to extend such credit while simultaneously protecting the small farmer against his own improvidence.[16]   Especially during the 1930's the peasant's desire for cheap credit had other origins as well as plans to add to the nation's agricultural capital; among these origins were hopes of reducing a heavy interest burden, paying existing debt, spending more on consumption, and acquiring already developed farm land.   Much discussion of peasant problems concerned "rural reconstruction," where the distinction between development and reform is tenuous indeed.[17]

1940-47

During and immediately after the war years there was much talk of postwar planning.   The most comprehensive statement of government planning was the Board of Ministers' 1946 *Post-war Development Proposals*.   In the introductory chapter the Ministers stressed the great need for increased savings to push through the desired volume of investment.   ". . . the immediate postwar rate of savings is absolutely inadequate for any ambitious scheme of development.   Much greater savings have to be forthcoming to make the proposed schemes successful."   Moreover, continued the Ministers, the proposed schemes themselves represented a careful selection of the most promising development projects.   Ceylon should not attempt immediately to push development along all lines.   The island's natural and human resources required that initial emphasis be placed upon agriculture, education, and health rather than upon manufacturing; the major industrial push should come later, after Ceylon's economy had been developed in preparatory ways.   However, since Ceylon could not achieve a satisfactory income through agriculture alone, manufacturing development would have to come,

[16] See, for example, B. B. Das Gupta, "Land Mortgage Credit," *Ceylon Economic Journal*, II (March, 1930), 41-58; J. A. Mabin, "Cooperative Land Mortgage Banks," *Ceylon Economic Journal*, VI (Dec., 1934), 2-11; B. B. Das Gupta, "The Reorganisation of Mortgage Credit Agencies," *Ceylon Economic Journal*, VII (Dec., 1935), 40-49.

[17] See *Report on Rural Reconstruction in Ceylon*.

and some immediate progress should be attempted in such industries as fertilizer and textiles—but not in heavy industries for which the island's natural resources were not suited.[18]

First priority, the Ministers advised, should be placed on staple foods and other locally needed commodities that can be produced "with reasonable efficiency." ". . . between two equally promising plans" the government should choose that "which allows itself to be adjusted most readily to unforeseen external conditions." Moreover, plantation agriculture is not likely to expand as in predepression days. ". . . no development in tea and rubber and possibly in coconuts can be expected."[19]

Finances for postwar development, argued the Ministers, should come from both the government and private enterprise. Ceylon should acquire the domestic and foreign funds needed for the proposed program via increased savings and export trade balances, the latter to be achieved through import reductions and stable export revenues. Such a cautious policy might delay plans, but foreign loans were much too costly to be the main emphasis, and expenditure on foreign machinery would not yield the same secondary benefits as local spending. The Ministers added that they did not wish import quotas to remain as restrictive as they were in the immediate postwar period, since such quotas might permanently damage the incentive to reduce costs and improve quality, and might result in inflation rather than an increased volume of real savings.[20]

In its 1946 *Report on Industrial Development and Policy* the Executive Committee of Labour, Industry and Commerce was more anxious than the Board of Ministers to get on with the job of manufacturing development. The Committee was impressed by statistical estimates showing that per-capita incomes were higher within industrial than agricultural countries, and higher within industrial than agricultural sections of both industrial and agricultural countries. Presumably the Committee's members also agreed with the arguments spelled out by the Acting Director of Industries in a 1947 report.[21] International trade barriers and the threat of

[18] *Postwar Development Proposals* (Colombo: Government Record Office, 1946), pp. 12-15, 36, 40, 42, 49.
[19] *Ibid.*, pp. 35-37.
[20] *Ibid.*, pp. 49-50.
[21] *Report on Industrial Development and Policy*, pp. 13-14; *New State-Owned Factories* (Sessional Paper XXIII, 1947), p. 4.

future wars, argued the Acting Director, made it essential for every country to have a balanced economy, with an adequate industrial sector; the terms of international trade had turned against Ceylon; industrial development would enable Ceylonese to gain additional income by processing the island's raw materials; new factories would provide new employment. The Executive Committee accepted both the "infant industry" and the "unfair competition" arguments for protection. "All industrially advanced countries . . . and new industrial countries . . . have adopted the principle of protection to encourage industries . . . protection is also sometimes given to established industries to withstand competition, usually of an unfair nature."[22]

In other parts of their 1946 *Report* the Executive Committee explained in some detail the reasons for classifying various industries as "basic" and reserving them for state enterprise:

In coming to the conclusion that basic industries should be State monopolies we are influenced by three main considerations. Firstly, basic industries occupy positions of strategic value in the development of industrial resources, so that their output and price levels acquire a national significance. Secondly, by their nature these industries are ones that have all the probabilities of becoming monopolies, and supplying as they do the basic needs of the community they will be socially important. Thirdly, the industries in question require a large capital outlay, which in the circumstances it is best that the State should provide.[23]

The Minister of Labour, Industry and Commerce had earlier explained what was perhaps an even more fundamental reason for relying heavily on government enterprise. Thus, in 1939: ". . . we will make all the investigations and then offer it [the industrial project] to the public to take it up if they are ready and they like it; but if they do not do so because they are afraid to undertake these new ventures, then I say it is the duty of Government to step in and undertake them and show the way for future expansion." In 1940: ". . . people are so unused to industrial enterprise that they get cold feet before they start an enterprise." "There is unfortunately a great dearth of industrial enterprise among the public." In their 1946 *Report* the Executive Committee of Labour, Industry and

[22] *Report on Industrial Development and Policy*, pp. 23-26.
[23] *Ibid.*, pp. 18-19.

Commerce placed special emphasis on private enterprise's failure to respond to proposals to set up a plywood factory: "This decision had a bearing on subsequent Government policy towards industrial development."[24]

Among Ceylonese wartime periodicals, the *Ceylon Industrial and Trade Recorder* had the most to say about economic development. In a series entitled "Points on Economic Planning" contributor "John Citizen" argued for planned diversification, attention to the relative scarcities of different resources, and balanced growth. "Excessive specialization in the use of factors of production within a country, prevents . . . adaptation or makes it slow and painful." Hence Ceylon should seek "diversification of employment opportunities with the extension of primary production to the neighbouring higher stages of production." But industries in Ceylon should not be the highly mechanized affairs that they are in Western countries. "In a country that does not make machinery and where labour is unemployed, for what purpose do we *save* labour?" Moreover, planners should remember that a rise in Ceylonese incomes will increase the demand for imports unless local consumer suppliers satisfy the increased demand. Expenditure on public works and the like must be co-ordinated "with the development of suitable consumption goods industries," also with expanded production of essential building materials.[25]

Concerning the state's role in industrial development, the *Ceylon Industrial and Trade Recorder* argued: "As was the case in several other countries, Government had to play the role of pioneer of industry in Ceylon. . . . But Government activity alone in this sphere will not suffice, and Government cannot for long burden itself with numerous industrial undertakings. . . ." ". . . there should be a close association between the Government and industry at every stage of development . . . akin to partnership in industry."[26]

Among pre-1947 academic writings the most nearly complete theory of development was that in C. Suriyakumaran, *Ceylon, Beveridge and Bretton Woods.* An ardent advocate of planned

[24] *State 1939*, p. 3115; *1940*, pp. 1642, 1652; *Report on Industrial Development and Policy*, p. 8.
[25] *Ceylon Industrial and Trade Recorder*, March, 1945, p. 10; May 1945, pp. 8-10, 15.
[26] *Ibid.*, March, 1945, p. 3.

industrial growth, Suriyakumaran based his argument on rural underemployment and the unstable market for Ceylon's dominant export
crops.   Policies which he recommended included protection and
subsidized government enterprise.   Because of underemployment,
Suriyakumaran pointed out, business costs and economic costs may
not coincide.   If unemployment is the alternative to factory jobs,
new industries may add to real national income even when value
of output is less than expense incurred.   Moreover, because of
"fundamental disequilibrium" in the balance of international payments, the Adam Smith argument for "international division of
labour based mainly on differences in natural resources will not
hold."   Industrial countries have greater bargaining power in
international trade, so that agricultural countries are likely to suffer
continual payments deficits.[27]

Like "John Citizen," Suriyakumaran asked for balanced growth.
Industrialization could not come, he argued, by concentrating on
hydroelectric power and transportation and expecting the rest of the
economy to respond.   The higher incomes resulting from such
projects would merely lead to an increased demand for imports
unless Ceylonese suppliers simultaneously turned out increased
quantities of many goods.   ". . . the industries on which the 'new'
demand is to operate must be simultaneously existing or created."
Fortunately, rapid and balanced growth was not beyond Ceylon's
potentialities.   "The Economics of Expansion, agricultural and industrial—is not so difficult as Blimpish-financiers may make out.
What seems difficult to produce in Ceylon seems to be confidence and
honest determination."   Russia's Five Year Plans showed what an
underdeveloped, largely agricultural country could quickly accomplish.[28]

1947-1956

Since the United National party that won the 1947 election
represented about the same groups that had dominated the State
Council, the development theory which the Cabinet expounded
during the first several years of full independence differed little
from that which the Board of Ministers had endorsed in *Postwar*

[27] C. Suriyakumaran, *Ceylon, Beveridge and Bretton Woods*, pp. 19-23, 35-40.
[28] *Ibid.*, pp. 23-27, 49-50, 68.

Development Proposals. Speeches reiterated, added details to, and sometimes slightly modified the Board's 1946 reasoning.

One constantly repeated theme was the government's inability to shoulder the whole burden of development. Another often recurring argument referred to the vicious circle hindering development in a poor country: the need for greater savings to finance the investments required for economic progress, but the difficulty of securing adequate savings before progress raised incomes. Cabinet spokesmen therefore concluded that an ambitious development program required much aid from private investment and foreign capital. Although the U. N. P. characterized its program as "practical socialism," many Cabinet speeches during 1947-52 assigned greater roles to private enterprise and foreign firms than did the government's specific policy decisions, which defined "basic" (or state-reserved) industries very broadly and looked rather coldly at would-be foreign investors. This was true even in the years when the Finance Minister stated most explicitly his belief that Ceylon could effectively use newly created money to finance development works and maintain full employment.[29]

Speeches and policies on the whole coincided when the subject was the pattern of development sought. Statements as well as outlays gave a higher priority to agricultural than to industrial development, also displayed belief that much economic progress would come through more widespread education and improved health. Among the reasons which Cabinet spokesmen gave for their policies were the vast areas of potentially cultivable land and the current lack of an "industrial tradition" and needed industrial skills.[30]

Because of the 1947-52 discrepancy between the encouragement of private investment and foreign firms given in speeches and in policies, post-1952 policy statements did not show as great a change as the policies themselves. Government statements during 1954-55 did, however, place greater stress on foreign enterprise, private investment, and cottage industries than did the earlier speeches. The leading statements of U. N. P. development theory during this

---

[29] See, *inter alia, House, 1947-48* V. 1, c. 418-26, 1629-30; *1948-49*, V. 3, c. 1053, 1226, 1856-63; V. 4, c. 1322; V. 5, c. 2089-90; *1949-50*, V. 6, c. 131-36, 1209; *1950-51*, v. 8, c. 652-53; *1952-53*, v. 12, c. 652; International Bank Mission, *op. cit.*, pp. 507-17.

[30] See, *inter alia, House, 1947-48*, V. 1, c. 1348, 1402, 1405; *1948-49*, v. 3, c. 1052, 1063, 1856; *1949-50*, V. 6, c. 1220.

period were the Minister of Finance's budget speech of July 1954, the Minister of Industries' policy speech of September 1954, and the Planning Secretariat's 1955 volume on the Six-Year Programme.

Minister of Finance Jayawardene stressed the influence of Ceylon's foreign balances upon budgetary policy and pointed out that an ambitious development program financed through newly created credit would further reduce these balances and bring about price inflation. Current expenditures, he argued, would have to be slashed so that development outlays could be continued. Government subsidies to consumers could not take precedence over capital formation.[31]

Minister of Industries Vaithianathan thought Ceylon's pre-1954 lack of industrial success attributable to "insufficient encouragement offered to private enterprise, excessive mechanization and overcapitalization and the types of goods selected for manufacture." With respect to the first fault: "It is an axiom that one of the strongest human motives in regard to all private industry is the profit motive." Successful state enterprise requires harsh compulsions. ". . . anywhere in a democracy, State-owned and State-managed industries do not prosper. . . . the first duty of Government is not to do things for which it is not well equipped but to get things done . . . . if Government creates a favorable climate and provides fertile soil, the innate urges, talents and ambitions of the individual in Ceylon would exceed many-fold anything the Government could hope to produce direct."[32]

Concerning excessive mechanization and overcapitalization, the Minister of Industries remarked: "Unfortunately, the people who come to this country to advise and plan our industries did not take into account the fact that we had a large labour force here. " ". . . our industrial policy needs to be readjusted to suit the conditions of Ceylon." He also disagreed with another set of foreign experts, the International Bank Mission, who had criticized Ceylon's development program as putting too much emphasis upon the domestic market and too little upon the possibilities of further export. "More than one-third of our privately employed industrial labour," he complained, "is engaged in producing goods for the foreign market.

[31] *House, 1954-55,* v. 18, c. 4-38.
[32] *Senate, 1954-55,* v. 8, c. 668-72.

. . . Instead of these, we should embark on the production of sugar, textiles, kitchen utensils, household goods . . . and tiles."[33]

In the *Six-Year Programme of Investment* the Planning Secretariat published a fairly complete statement of its development theory as well as an account and defense of specific planned outlays. "The general outlines of the economic problem facing Ceylon," it began,

are now familiar and do not need detailed elaboration. Population growth in the country has been exceptionally rapid in recent years whilst average standards of living remain relatively low. The broad solution to this problem is an expansion in the productive capacity of the economy. The rate of such an expansion must be sufficiently rapid not merely to keep pace with but also to outstrip population growth.

An expansion of the economy is also the solution to many of the ancillary problems which arise . . . . It is mainly a process of expansion that can provide increased employment to the additional population . . . [the] long run solution to the problem of instability . . . a means to a better distribution of income . . . .[34]

"Two of the most significant means of bringing about an expansion in output," the Planning Secretariat continued, "are simple improvements in methods of production on the one hand, and a higher volume of investment on the other. The scope for increasing output through improvements in methods is particularly large during the early stages of development specially in such spheres as agriculture. Improvements of this kind do not usually involve large quantities of capital. They are, therefore, of particular importance in countries where capital is scarce." But such improvements can "go only part of the way towards increasing output. The problem of expanding output is, therefore, in large measure a problem of increasing investment."[35]

Because of Ceylon's poverty, the Planning Secretariat argued, government policy should seek to attract foreign as well as private funds. Expanded local investment should come chiefly from increased savings out of income as it rises, and from utilization of the island's unemployed labor and other resources, rather than from a lowering of Ceylon's already low level of consumption. "Unemployed labour may, for instance, be applied to such types of basic

---

[33] *Ibid.*, c. 673-78.
[34] *Six-Year Programme of Investment*, p. 3.
[35] *Ibid.*, pp. 5-6.

capital as roads, dams and buildings," also "community benefit and rural development projects, which apply voluntary labour to capital works." Moreover, since Ceylon was labor-rich and capital-poor, investments undertaken should embody "labour intensive techniques" when such techniques did not involve loss of efficiency.[36]

In explaining the pattern of outlays projected under the Six-Year Programme, the Planning Secretariat pointed out that "a programme of investment for the Government must be fashioned on the basis of a pattern of priorities appropriate to the public sector," not "with a system of priorities suitable for the economy as a whole." Hence the small outlay projected for manufacturing. "The objective is . . . to promote industrial development through the private sector. The Government's [industrial] programme is, therefore, confined to such requirements as are ancillary to this objective." State outlays must, however, provide for "utility services and basic overheads of the economy as a whole," whose "importance to a process of development can seldom be exaggerated," since their "absence reduces the efficiency of production and raises costs."[37]

Criteria to which the Planning Secretariat referred when explaining their choice of projects included diversification so as to make the economy less susceptible to changes in foreign markets, balance between consumer-goods and producer-goods industries, local availability of raw materials, and the already mentioned capital-labor ratio. "The Government will give special emphasis to the development of small-scale industries. These industries may be specially suitable in conditions where capital is scarce and labour is plentiful."[38]

Protectionist measures were believed to be necessary, but also a threat. "In the initial stages of industrialization it will be necessary to wean consumers away from imports to locally produced substitutes." But: "Quality should not be allowed to suffer as, otherwise, the Government would be protecting inefficient industry and forcing the Ceylon consumer to buy low quality products while weakening the competitive power of such products abroad." Like legislators and journalists who saw that protection would at least initially injure the consumer, the Planning Secretariat spoke only of effect on quality, not also of the effect on price.

[36] *Ibid.*, pp. 6-8.
[37] *Ibid.*, pp. 11-13.
[38] *Ibid.*, pp. 28, 238-39, 470-71.

Foreign exchange needs in the proposed program were to be covered in part through the attraction of foreign capital, in part through a surplus of exports over imports plus income transfers abroad. The Planning Secretariat argued that Ceylon should build up its foreign balances in boom years and draw them down in bad, so as to keep the level of investment free from fluctuations in the terms of trade.[39]

Most technical economic analysis in the *Six-Year Programme* was presumably that of economist Gamani Corea, who served as Planning Chief. Corea had, some years earlier, expressed other elements of the development theory which he believed applicable to Ceylon. "Advances of a slow and piecemeal nature," he wrote, "may in the end frustrate themselves. Improvement in the social services tends to encourage population growth." But Corea favored initial emphasis upon agriculture. ". . . where undeveloped cultivable land is still available the opening up and working of these areas by economic units of production is an obvious first step. . . . In the context of the Ceylon economy there is a further important reason as to why agricultural development is almost a prerequisite for industrial growth. Almost all industrial projects today require machines and other capital equipment that can only be obtained from abroad. Hence the sooner we are able to replace food imports by imports of capital goods through our own food production, the faster is the probable rate of industrial development."[40]

"It is likely," Corea continued, "that new enterprise coming into being in a developing economy will tend generally to be of two types; on the one hand new industries would tend to arise that produce commodities for which markets already exist in a country but which are supported by imports. . . . On the other hand, there may be a tendency for industries to grow which are chiefly concerned with the processing of products already cultivated or manufactured in the country, but exported in a comparatively raw state." Ceylon's small market hindered development of the former type. ". . . the scope of economic enterprise is naturally small in a society where markets are small due to the poverty of the people." The task

[39] *Ibid.*, pp. 46-47, 63-64, 244-45.
[40] Gamani Corea, "Some Problems of Economic Development in Ceylon," *Ceylon Economist*, I (Aug., 1950), 41-42.

is to escape the vicious circle: low incomes, therefore small markets, therefore low incomes.[41]

"It would seem," Corea concluded, "that borrowing from abroad is an unavoidable necessity for a developing country whose standards of living are too small to allow an adequate volume of savings and whose resources are too limited to provide, within its frontiers, all its varied requirements in capital equipment." ". . . a developing country is usually most desirous to foster industries that could provide the country with its own needs. It may however be difficult to persuade foreign firms to interest themselves in ventures producing for the home market."[42]

E. B. Tisseverasinghe, Assistant Secretary to the Minister of Industries, also published thoughts about the island's economic progress, contributing three articles which developed further some of the points which the Minister raised in his September, 1954, speech. "A competitive factory industry on the scale which it has reached in advanced countries just cannot exist in Ceylon," wrote Tisseverasinghe. "The alternatives left are then either small-scale industry or no industry at all, since the field is not one for which pure home [cottage] industry is equipped." "What to produce is quite readily discovered from the Customs Returns. Ceylon imports about Rs. 1700 millions worth of goods, and it is estimated that at least Rs. 700 millions of this is within the eventual capacity of small-scale industry."[43]

The Assistant Secretary rejected the argument that agricultural underemployment pointed to the need for huge irrigation projects in the Dry Zone or massive industrialization. Three acres of paddy land, he argued, was the maximum which could be efficiently cultivated with the use of intensive techniques; thus the total acreage required was less than that under cultivation in 1946. Land redistribution and agricultural reform were the prime needs.[44]

B. B. Das Gupta, the Central Bank's Director of Economic Research, stressed the island's lack of entrepreneurship:

[41] *Ibid.*, pp. 43-44.
[42] *Ibid.*, pp. 47, 51.
[43] E. B. Tisseverasinghe, "The Scope of Small Industry in Ceylon," *New Lanka*, VI (Oct., 1954), 25-31.
[44] E. B. Tisseverasinghe, "The Pattern of Occupation in Idealized Ceylon," *New Lanka*, VI (Jan., 1955), 47-59; "The Content of Employment in Industry," *New Lanka*, VI (April, 1955), 36-43.

. . . market deficiency, though important, does not seem to be the root cause of the stagnation of the region. Actually, production has not even risen to the level of the existing market; the potential market, of course, lies completely untapped. The root cause would seem to lie on the supply side, in factor scarcity. There is, of course, no scarcity of labour and land, on the contrary even much of what is available remains idle or under-used. But there is a great shortage of capital and entrepreneurship. In the literature on economic development, the capital shortage has been much high-lighted, but not so much as the entrepreneur shortage. Yet it seems to be no less serious a handicap. . . . How else can we possibly explain the fact that, even when capital, technical skills and markets all are assured, as for instance, in the case of many small-scale industries catering for domestic demand, new enterprises are still not coming into existence. . . ? It is not easy to see how this entrepreneur shortage can be overcome. Education can do much, but the best school for businessmen is business itself. It is by moving in the business world that one gets one's knowledge and ideas. Here . . . we have the familiar vicious circle.[45]

With respect to Ceylon's other major lack, Das Gupta concluded: ". . . the capital situation and outlook does not seem to be as hope-less as it is often made out. A small amount of capital is already available." Taxation, he thought, could provide additional capital as incomes rose, and credit creation could help if used cautiously so as to avoid inflation and drain of foreign balances. With respect to foreign capital: "Provided it is obtained on reasonable non-exploita-tion terms and in sufficient quantities, nothing obviously will be better."[46]

Among the island's professional economists, N. K. Sarkar was perhaps the most confident that a resolute government could achieve rapid development and that industrialization was the most effective route to higher incomes. "Once we start industrialisation at a high tempo," he wrote, "the income generated thereby will increase cumu-latively, so that the supply of funds for further development and expansion of social services will not become scarce. The decisive question, therefore, is to start capital development at *a high tempo.*" Official development programs so far had been much too small and weak. ". . . the natural inertia of the present situation smothered the

[45] B. B. Das Gupta, "The Theory and Reality of Economic Development," *Central Bank of Ceylon Bulletin*, Nov., 1955, pp. 10-14.
[46] *Ibid.*

weak and half-hearted efforts that the government was making."[47]

One major reason which Sarkar gave for his industrial emphasis was the large volume of underemployed labor on the island. Surplus farmers could, he argued, become productive manufacturing employees and thus add to national income. Primarily a population economist, he believed that agricultural expansion in the Dry Zone would be "merely a postponement of the issue" represented by Ceylon's rapid population growth, since to transplant village life to the Dry Zone would be to keep human fertility high.[48]

University students in large part shared Sarkar's high estimate of potential industrial progress. "The average undergraduate," wrote ex-Professor B. B. Das Gupta in 1952, "has almost a religious faith in industrialization."[49] In Parliament and in polemical writings, the most consistent support for rapid industrialization came from the Left. Trotskyist leader Colvin R. de Silva argued that further agricultural development depended upon mechanized farming and balanced industrialization. The agricultural producer, he reasoned, must sell his surplus produce to an industrial population. Trotskyist leader N. M. Perera expressed essentially the same argument and stressed the "multiplier" effect of rising development expenditures upon consumer income and outlay. In the absence of balanced industrialization, he stated, development spending would swell the demand for consumer imports and thus drain foreign balances. Communist leader Pieter Keuneman referred to Sarkar's argument that Ceylon's surplus agricultural labor could supply the real resources needed for an industrialization program.[50]

Legislative leaders of the Sri Lanka Freedom party did not, to the same extent as the United National party and Left spokesmen, enunciate a development theory. In general, their speeches reflected substantial distrust of foreign capital, a greater faith than the post-1953 U. N. P.'s in government enterprise, and greater concern with

[47] N. K. Sarkar, "The Budget Debate," *Ceylon Economist*, II (Sept., 1951), 51-56.

[48] N. K. Sarkar, special articles in *Ceylon Daily News* of Sept. 20, 27; Oct. 4, 11, 18, 25; November 1, 8—all of 1954. Also see Mr. Sarkar's unpublished doctoral thesis, "Demography of Ceylon in the Twentieth Century" (London School of Economics, 1954), chaps. x and xi.

[49] B. B. Das Gupta, book review, *University of Ceylon Review*, X (April, 1952), 184.

[50] See, *inter alia*, House, *1947-48*, v. 1, c. 920-21, 1382; v. 2, c. 2882; *1948-49*, v. 3, c. 1578, 1816; *1954-55*, v. 20, c. 570-73; *1955-56*, v. 21, c. 985.

peasant agriculture than industrial problems.[51]   This last view was not shared by some of the Leftist elements which joined with the S. L. F. P. to form the People's United Front; but the 1956 election platform reflected S. L. F. P. thought in this respect.[52]   As Chapter IV has stated, the new Cabinet apparently has rejected the reasoning which led the post-1953 U. N. P. to stress cottage industries.

[51] See, *inter alia, House, 1952-53*, v. 12, c. 1325-36, 1558-72, 1758-88, 3174-76, 3849-50; *1953-54*, v. 14, c. 188-209; v. 15, c. 995-97; *1954-55*, v. 18, c. 1375-77.

[52] See *Free Lanka*, Jan. 8, 1956, p. 3; March 11, 1956, p. 3.

6

Effects of Nationalist Sentiment and Government Policies on Ceylonese Income

INCOME ESTIMATES AND INCOME TRENDS

As IN MOST "underdeveloped" economies, so in Ceylon income data are inadequate and sometimes inconsistent. The two major difficulties are securing reasonably accurate figures for the volume and value of nonexport production, and calculating a reasonably representative price index to use in deflating monetary totals. Since much of Ceylon's population lives by peasant agriculture, the former difficulty is formidable enough. But controversy over the price deflator also has led to widely differing estimates of income movements. The Planning Secretariat, apparently using some compromise between the official cost-of-living index and the import-price index as its deflator, shows per capita income for 1948 and 1949 well above the 1938 level. The Ministry of Finance, apparently using import prices to adjust the monetary totals, states that per capita income did not rise above the 1938 level until 1950.[1]

There are no income estimates for the 1920's and most of the 1930's. But since Ceylon has depended heavily upon imports, their record may enable a rough comparison; when discussing changes in the level of consumer welfare, the Ministry of Finance has based calculations on per-capita imports of consumer goods.[2] The degree of postwar income rise indicated by the import record alone does not

---

[1] See *Six-Year Programme of Investment*, p. 4; *Economic and Social Development of Ceylon*, pp. 31, 36. There has long been controversy over the merits of the official cost of living index. See, *inter alia*, papers by N. K. Sarkar and K. Williams in the *University of Ceylon Review*, VII (Oct., 1949), 302-23; VIII (Jan., 1950), 56-59; also comments in *Economic and Social Development of Ceylon*, pp. 34-37. A 1949-50 study showed that imports were then 43 per cent of the average working-class family's budget (*ibid.*, p. 36).

[2] *Economic and Social Development of Ceylon*, pp. 34-37.

TABLE I
INCOME ESTIMATES, 1938-1954

| | NATIONAL INCOME (Millions of Rupees) | | | INCOME PER CAPITA (Rupees) | | | PRICE INDICES† | |
| | Planning Secretariat* | | Ministry of Finance† | Planning Secretariat* | Calculated from Ministry of Finance† | | Official Cost-of-Living | Import |
Year	Current Prices	1938 Prices	Current Prices	1938 Prices	Via Official Cost-of-Living Index (1938-39 Prices)	Via Import-Price Index (1934-38 Prices)	(Nov. 1938-Apr. 1939= 100)	(1934-38 =100)
1938	596	596	652	102	112	110	100‡	102
1947	2509	732	2608	106	150	92	252	413
1948	2799	929	2879	131	156	91	260	443
1949	3013	978	3056	134	162	96	258	423
1950	3796	1115	3958	148	193	121	272	434
1951	4527	1269	4619	164	211	116	283	514
1952	4441	1238	4507	156	202	103	281	554
1953	4419	1218	4479	149	192	109	286	505
1954	....	....	4800§	...	201	129	284	443

* Source: *Six-Year Programme of Investment*, p. 4.
† Source: *Economic and Social Development of Ceylon*, pp. 31, 61.
‡ Index for Nov. 1938-April 1939.
§ Preliminary estimate.

differ greatly from the degree of increase calculated when estimated monetary income is deflated by import prices, and the discrepancy between the two records seems to be largely explained by Ceylon's increasing reliance upon domestically produced rice.[3] Per-capita imports fell slightly between 1926 and 1938; these years included the "depression decade."

Both the income totals and the import figures are of course affected by the terms of trade. What Ceylon can buy depends upon the prices of exports and imports. But neither between 1926 and 1954, nor between 1938 and 1954 has there been any pronounced trend change in these terms. Sharp fluctuations have taken place, but the favorable and unfavorable changes have largely offset each other during the longer periods. Thus the trend rise in per-capita income seems to be attributable to increased "real production" on the island.

Such output data as are available indicate that production has advanced somewhat more rapidly than imports, but not as rapidly as the more optimistic income estimates. In other words, "real output" per capita is probably not so very much greater than in 1926

[3] *Ibid.*, pp. 64-65. The record for both income and imports probably would look somewhat better if it included 1955 figures.

TABLE II
POPULATION AND IMPORT INDICES, 1926-1954

Year	Estimated* Population at Mid-Year	Population Index	Imports		Consumption* Imports Per Capita
			Total Volume*	Imports Per Capita	
	(000's)	(1938=100)	(1934-38=100)	Col. 3÷Col. 2	(1938=100)
1926	4928	85	84	99	.....
1928	5091	87	95	109	106.9
1933	5419	93	81	87	88.2
1938	5826	100	98	98	100.0
1941	6044	104	93	90	92.7
1944	6308	108	67	61	88.0
1947	6903	118	108	92	104.1
1948	7109	122	110	90	95.8
1949	7321	126	119	94	99.9
1950	7544	129	133	103	106.6
1951	7742	133	149	112	119.5
1952	7940	136	152	112	121.4
1953	8155	140	158	113	119.8
1954	8385†	144	157	109	105.5

* Source: *Economic and Social Development of Ceylon*, pp. 36, 59, 61.
† Preliminary estimate.

TABLE III
TERMS OF TRADE, 1926-1954
(1934-38=100)

Year	Import Price Index	Export Price Index	Year	Import Price Index	Export Price Index
1926	194	193	1948	443	305
1928	183	141	1949	423	324
1933	98	71	1950	434	439
1938	102	99	1951	514	534
1941	147	133	1952	554	415
1944	349	190	1953	505	424
1947	413	300	1954	443	473

Source: *Economic and Social Development of Ceylon*, p. 61.

or 1938. Population rose by some 70 per cent during 1926-54, by 44 per cent during 1938-54. Exports, which measure the production of the plantation economy and its urban adjuncts, failed to keep up with population during the longer period, rising by only 63 per cent; during 1938-54 they rose somewhat more rapidly than population, or by 57 per cent.[4] Less can be said about the other sectors of the

[4] *Ibid.*, pp. 59, 61.

economy; the over-all trend seems to have been more favorable, but not dramatically so. Acreage cultivated in paddy, the peasants' mainstay, showed little increase between 1926 and 1945, when there began a rise that by 1954 had added one-sixth to the total area. Paddy-production estimates, which do not go back before 1944, and which may not be very accurate for subsequent years, show a doubling of output between 1945 and 1954.[5] Urban services might show a rather favorable record, if adequate statistics were available. Higher education, health, motor transportation, and banking are among the areas where advance seems to have been comparatively rapid. On the other hand, industrial output, except for the plantation exports, remained a small percentage of national income throughout the period, so that even if its growth had been more rapid than seems to have been the case, it could not have enabled per-capita production to rise very much.[6]

Income and production assignable to Ceylonese rather than to foreign residents and absentee shareholders must have grown somewhat more rapidly than total income and total production over the period, as the degree of Ceylonization increased in public employment, on the plantations, and in various other parts of the economy. There are no data which allow a quantitative assessment of Ceylonization's effects. Per-capita figures probably were not greatly affected, although the trend was highly important for those Ceylonese nationals who moved in to the better jobs and received profits from their new enterprises.

Income and luxury taxes also helped to divert income from foreign to Ceylonese nationals, likewise from higher-income to lower-income families regardless of nationality. But not all the distributional changes seem to have favored the poor. Population increase in the peasant sector continually cut the average size of the cultivated plot and swelled the volume of landlessness; higher yields per acre and supplementary income from jobs outside the village often did not provide an adequate offset. There are no studies which clearly show how peasant incomes have moved over the years; but ap-

[5] *Ibid.*, pp. 64-65.
[6] During 1951-53 domestically produced industrial products (factory and cottage) consumed in Ceylon were only about 10 per cent of gross national product (*ibid.*, p. 129).

parently much, if not all, of the rise in per-capita income has gone to urban and plantation-sector groups.[7]

VARIABLES GOVERNING CEYLONESE INCOMES

Obviously, Ceylon's income and production records are not entirely attributable to government policy. Some of the most important variables governing income have been largely or wholly beyond Colombo's control: for example, foreign sales and purchase markets, natural resources, size of population, and cultural traits.

Since the terms of foreign trade did not show much trend change over such long periods as 1926-54 and 1938-54, it may appear at first glance as if movements in foreign markets had no appreciable effect on the trend in Ceylonese income and production. But this is not a justifiable conclusion. The terms of trade showed approximate trend constancy in spite of restrictions on tea and rubber acreage which themselves resulted from unfavorable turns in the export market. Had the market for Ceylonese exports remained as favorable as it was in the mid-twenties, plantation acreage and output would have been somewhat larger in later years.[8] Moreover, if plantation and related urban incomes had not fallen so sharply during the 1930's, commercial and industrial investments would almost surely have been greater, per-capita income would today be higher, and Ceylon would be better supplied with the labor, managerial, and entrepreneurial skills and attitudes required for commercial and industrial advance.

Import and export prices are of course not entirely beyond Ceylon's control. Agreement with other tea- and rubber-producing countries enabled the prices of those commodities to be held above the levels that otherwise would have prevailed. Rice-rubber negotiations with Communist China gave Ceylon somewhat more favorable terms than those quoted in the world market. Moreover, govern-

---

[7] Sample surveys are available for various years, including 1936-38, 1950-51, and 1953. Findings for 1936-38 are reprinted in Sir Ivor Jennings, *The Economy of Ceylon*, pp. 52-62. For the later years see *Final Report on the Economic Survey of Rural Ceylon, 1950-51* (Sessional Paper XI, 1954); and *Survey of Ceylon's Consumer Finances* (Colombo: Central Bank of Ceylon, 1954). In 1955 N. K. Sarkar and S. J. Tambiah of the University of Ceylon conducted a survey of villages in the Kandyan area.

[8] The market for rubber was more favorable during the earlier twenties, but the price falls that led to rubber acreage restriction were not great enough to prevent the planting of new areas.

ment policy can decrease—and the some extent has decreased—the significance of foreign trade for the Ceylonese economy, by making the island more nearly self-sufficient. But Ceylon's present economic structure and its apparent potentialities are such that no rapid swing towards self-sufficiency, regardless of its pattern, seems to have a chance of raising real incomes. In the foreseeable future, foreign markets will remain very important determinants of Ceylonese economic welfare.

Ceylon's natural resources are, by definition, completely independent of government policy, although policy can change the rate and the efficiency of their exploitation. On the whole, Ceylon is not well endowed with natural resources.[9] Its Wet Zone lowlands and central highlands can give high agricultural yields, but much of the island consists of Dry Zone jungle, which must be cleared, irrigated, and further prepared at high cost before it can become productive. Mineral resources are scanty and do not include coal or oil. Water power can be further developed, but its potentialities seem to be much more limited than optimists believed them to be in the 1920's.

Size of population has been, and is, in a sense, a variable highly subject to governmental influence. Government hospitals and sanitation measures have greatly reduced the death rate; the postwar antimalarial campaign was especially effective in this respect. But, as long as the government accepts health and lengthened life as policy goals, there is little it can do to slow population growth, which has carried the island from less than five million inhabitants in 1926 to nearly nine million by 1956. Even if subsidized birth-control clinics were politically feasible, decline in fertility would be quite slow. Other conceivable routes to a lower birth rate, such as the urbanization of rural families, also would be slow—and perhaps not feasible within the limits of Ceylon's economy.[10]

Malthusians can, however, exaggerate the unfavorable effects of population growth upon Ceylonese incomes. Especially in the past, improved health has increased labor efficiency and has in itself represented a welcome rise in "real income." Moreover, if people live longer, lifetime income per capita rises unless yearly income per

---

[9] See International Bank Mission, *op. cit.*; K. Kuluratnam, "Minerals and the Economic Development of Ceylon," *Ceylon Economist*, III (Sept., 1954), 11-26.

[10] For an opposite viewpoint, see N. K. Sarkar, "Demography of Ceylon in the Twentieth Century."

capita falls more rapidly than length of life rises. In Ceylon the Malthusian effect has not been nearly so unfavorable, although in many heavily populated agricultural districts annual income per capita may be appreciably lower than in earlier decades.

Cultural traits, the remaining variable mentioned above, have apparently been no more favorable than the other variables for a rapid advance in production and income. Numerous speeches and writings have stressed traits hindering economic progress: e.g., adherence to customary methods of production, appreciation of leisure, consumer attitudes and customs that depress saving and investment, and the lack of commercial and industrial traditions which develop worker and managerial skills, efficiency-increasing attitudes, and the "spirit of enterprise."[11] Like size of population, these traits are not entirely beyond government influence, and apparently the government has achieved some success in these respects through schools, the rural reconstruction program, the state's own commercial ventures, and various aids and encouragements given to co-operatives and private investors. But if cultural traits are not entirely independent of governmental control, they at least seem to be very stubborn.[12]

NATIONALISM'S EFFECTS UPON CEYLONESE INCOMES

Nationalist sentiment is an income-determining variable which must be placed in a somewhat different category from foreign markets, natural resources, population growth, and cultural traits. It has itself been an influence on some foreign markets and Ceylonese cultural traits and, of course, upon government policies. More specifically, nationalism has affected Ceylonese incomes through re-

[11] See *Six-Year Programme of Investment*, p. 201; International Bank Mission, *op. cit.*, pp. 225-26, 522-24; P. T. Ellsworth, "Factors in the Development of Ceylon," *American Economic Review*, XLIII (May, 1953), 15-25; Sir Ivor Jennings, *The Economy of Ceylon*, pp. 33-37, 101-05, 184-86.

[12] Critics from the Right have argued that some government policies have decreased efficiency and enterprise by weakening the association between performance and reward and encouraging the public to leave too much to the state. Critics from the Left have argued that a vigorous government attack on the problem could bring about rapid cultural change. Whether this is possible, and whether it requires the sacrifice of other, major values, are questions perhaps best left to sociologists and political scientists with a profound understanding of the Ceylonese folk. The optimists who hold high hopes usually point to such examples as pre-1914 Japan, where the culture seems to have been better suited to rapid economic advance, and the Communist regimes in Russia and China.

strictionist, promotional, and fiscal policies; through foreign reactions to the nationalist movement; and through changes in the Ceylonese people's values and attitudes.

The last of these may well be the most important and certainly has served to raise Ceylonese incomes. But what needs to be said about it can be said very quickly. National self-awareness, combined with awareness of foreign wealth and power, has contributed to economic ambition and effort, qualities not conspicuously present in the easygoing culture of an earlier Ceylon. It has provided a widespread desire not only for personal gain but also for a greater Ceylon and a better life for other Ceylonese. Effort, however, has often taken unproductive forms, such as denouncing and exorcising foreign devils, rather than concentrating on efficient performance. Nationalist emotions have also encouraged overoptimism, or the undertaking of business and public projects where value of output has not covered cost.

Foreign reactions to Ceylonese nationalism have been clearly unfavorable to incomes on the island. Fears of hostile treatment have caused foreign capitalists and experts to raise the supply prices at which funds and skills have been made available. In so far as loan capital and technicians for government-sponsored projects are concerned, the International Bank, the Colombo Plan, and various United Nations agencies have largely nullified such unfavorable reactions, but schemes of international co-operation have so far not provided an adequate substitute for foreign private enterprise.

This statement, of course, rests in part upon certain judgments concerning Ceylonese private and governmental enterprise. If these could, with the aid of foreign loans and foreign exports, develop the island's resources as effectively as foreign firms, the absence of foreign equity capital would do no harm. But the record does not justify so optimistic a conclusion. Ceylonese entrepreneurs have been reluctant to open up new fields and have not displayed efficiency in the fields which they have entered. Government planners have not been fortunate in their selection of projects, and public management has been less efficient than private. Moreover, if nationalism did not arouse fears, foreign companies could supply funds and skills to supplement those which Ceylon might be able to secure in other ways.

Many Ceylonese, of course, challenge this entire line of reasoning and especially dispute the claim that foreign private enterprise can aid Ceylon.[13] Some merely praise national economic independence and denounce profits and salaries paid to foreigners. Others refer to the British record, described as exploitative in the manner explained above. Some of the more sophisticated make use of a lump-of-investment theory and complement it with an infant-industry argument.[14]

Foreign enterprise, they say, is financially strong and aggressive; Ceylonese enterprise is financially weak and conscious of its weakness. The Ceylonese market is small and often will not accommodate more than one or two firms. Thus, when a foreign company enters as a rival to an already existing local firm, it drives the latter out of business. If it enters an industry which a local firm was considering, it precludes the latter's entry. The very realization that foreign firms may later compete serves to paralyze Ceylonese entrepreneurs. But until local enterprise gains confidence, experience, and assets, the island cannot prosper. The government must reserve investment opportunities for its citizens.

There is much truth in this nationalist argument. In Ceylon the lump-of-investment theory holds to a greater extent than in such a country as the United States. Ceylonese capitalists are not very enterprising; if foreign rivals scare them away from one venture, they are not likely to turn immediately to another. Moreover, in the small Ceylonese market, the scale of investment is small, and a few new establishments are not likely to produce multiplier and accelerator effects leading to the creation of additional industry.

But the nationalists tend to misapply and overstress their argument. The very fact that Ceylonese capitalists are reluctant to enter new fields means that a policy of reserving opportunities for them is not likely to be a success; fear of foreign firms is not all that makes them timid. Furthermore, when capital flows in from abroad,

[13] See *House*, *1949-50*, v. 6, c. 1297; *1954-55*, v. 18, c. 961-62, 1322-23, 1377; *1955-56*, v. 21, c. 1021-22; *Ceylon Economist*, I (Nov., 1950), 111; III (Sept., 1954), 6-8.
[14] I have encountered this full argument only in oral discussions. Parts of it may be found in *State*, *1937*, pp. 664-66; *First Interim Report of the Technical Adviser on Industries*; and C. Loganathan, "Some Problems of the Ceylon Economy," *Ceylon Economist*, II (Second Quarter, 1952), 102-10.

it adds immediately to the volume of real resources available for Ceylon. Investment of local funds does not have this effect; it can only transfer resources from consumer use, or perhaps from idleness. Local investment can immediately produce needed foreign exchange only by reducing consumer imports. Finally, to keep out foreign firms is to protect inefficiency and to deny local men an opportunity to acquire skills as employees and associates of foreign management. Foreign companies can compete successfully in Ceylon not only because they are financially stronger than local rivals, but also because they know better how to insure quality and keep down cost. Government bureaus of standards and the like cannot provide such services for local firms.

A policy intended to raise Ceylonese incomes would logically exclude foreign enterprise only when:

(1) Existing Ceylonese firms are, or promise shortly to become, about as efficient as the foreign company is expected to be and the market is too small to accommodate an additional firm.

(2) Potential Ceylonese firms have just about completed plans for entry, their investment needs do not involve foreign exchange badly wanted for other purposes, and prospects of efficiency look good enough to justify giving them a trial period.

Even in these instances, Ceylon might gain through some sort of partnership between local and foreign enterprise that provides both additional capital and managerial skill. Moreover, policy makers should employ the infant-industry argument cautiously indeed when the problem is whether to exclude foreign enterprise. In its familiar form, the infant-industry argument calls for protection of domestic output, rather than local ownership. It dwells on the labor skills and ancillary industries that local production will develop —but these will develop more rapidly under foreign management if foreign management is more efficient.

As the discussion of national economic independence pointed out, actual government policy has been neither as moderate as that proposed here, nor as radical as fervent nationalists have desired. Rules have protected existing Ceylonese firms, almost without regard to their efficiency,[15] and have reserved some lines for potential local

[15] Various Ceylonese speakers and writers have bitterly criticized the government for allowing Bata to establish a branch plant for the manufacture of canvas-and-rubber shoes, since   a locally owned company was unable to withstand the

companies and the government itself. The government has allowed some foreign entry, however, and during most years Ceylon's Cabinets would have welcomed more new foreign companies, provided that they would enter industries which policy-makers sought to develop in this way, and provided that they would conform in other respects. The government program stressed partnership between foreign and local interests; overseas capital was to combine with local funds, and foreign management was to impart its "know-how."[16]

As has been stated, a few foreign companies entered under the program. A few others reportedly made offers that were rejected. It is impossible to say to what extent government policy by itself excluded foreign enterprise and to what extent overseas firms were scared off by fears of what might happen in the future. Very probably, specific restrictions have not kept out much capital; official exclusionism has not depressed Ceylon's income as much as the government's inability to convince foreign capitalists that future policy might not be much less friendly.[17]

In the case of foreign skills hired by existing foreign firms, the government's Ceylonization program, rather than the general political atmosphere, has been the more effective limiting agent. British businessmen have vigorously denounced the Ceylonization policy, stating that it decreases efficiency both by immediately raising costs

---

competition. See *House*, *1952-53*, v. 12 c. 3849-50; *1954-55*, v. 19, c. 2019; *Ceylon Observer*, Oct. 12, 1955, "Appeal to Patriotism"; *Ceylon Journal of Industry and Commerce*, Dec., 1952, p. 3; *Tribune*, July 22, 1955, p. 200. The International Bank Mission was critical of the government's delaying permission to Bata while the local factory "using more antiquated methods was given support." See International Bank Mission, *op. cit.*, pp. 516-17.

[16] For the rules prevailing during the last years of the U. N. P. regime, see *Government Policy in Respect of Private Investment in Ceylon* (July, 1955); also Minister Vaithianathan's speech, *Senate*, *1954-55*, v. 8, c. 679-81.

[17] A related problem here concerns the foreign capital already invested in Ceylon and the income which it and foreign residents receive. Exchange controls have so far allowed free conversion for capital and income payments to absentee owners and residents permanently leaving the island. Major reasons for this policy may have included fear that the British would cut imports or that Colombo Plan, International Bank, and other international aid would come to an end. The reason usually given for liberal conversion, however, is the hope that it will attract new foreign capital. So long as foreign investors are afraid to invest large sums except in forms and on terms which the government will not accept, the policy is in this respect bound to be a failure. Capital outflow has exceeded capital inflow and "current" remittances have averaged tens of millions of rupees yearly. The Left has frequently raised this point.

and by making long-range planning more uncertain.[18]   So far the rate of enforced replacement has been rather slow, however, and the record of plantation output and mercantile activity has been sufficiently good not to support a claim that Ceylonization has greatly depressed production.   It may have prevented some foreign commercial and industrial houses from expanding their business and may have made prospective new foreign firms more fearful of the future. On the opposite side of the ledger the government can of course point to the salaries transferred from foreigners to citizens and to the additional experience which Ceylonese have gained.

It is also difficult to reach any definite conclusion about the income-raising or -lowering effects of Ceylon's restrictions on import trade.   The island has pursued a protectionist policy, but the degree of protection afforded has been sufficiently moderate to make many nationalists ragingly object.[19]   Protective tariffs, quotas, and related devices have lowered quality and pushed up prices of various goods, but the government has not decided to raise import barriers high enough suddenly to multiply the number of industrial infants in the island's nursery.   Moreover, underemployment, as well as thoughts of infant-industry growth, obscures all income calculations.

Since underemployment on the island has been widespread, wages paid local workers and outlays for local materials have not always represented real social costs to Ceylon; at least sometimes the alternative has been idleness and disguised unemployment.   Customs duties lower than the margin between business and social costs raise, although they redistribute, real income on the island.[20]   But, unfortunately, neither policy-makers nor economists usually can measure social costs; neither foresight nor hindsight can say precisely when tariff rates are right.   Some protective measures undoubtedly have lowered real income: for example, denying import quotas to merchants until they have agreed also to stock local goods which consumers will not buy.   Other measures very probably have raised

---

[18] See the speech delivered by the Chairman of the Ceylon Chamber of Commerce at the Chamber's annual meeting, March 14, 1956; also see *Report of the Taxation Commission*, p. 83.

[19] See above, chap. ii, n. 42.

[20] For a Ceylonese argument based on this, see C. Suriyakumaran, *Ceylon, Beveridge and Bretton Woods*, chap. iv; also N. K. Sarkar, "Demography of Ceylon in the Twentieth Century," pp. 406, 439, 456, 468.

national income: for example, protection to cheap textiles largely produced by cottage crafts.

Similar reasoning, of course, applies to Ceylon's use of subsidies to become more nearly self-sufficient. Because of underemployment, a subsidy can be smaller than the margin between business and social costs. This almost certainly has been true of much rice production in newly irrigated lands, since labor has there been the major cost element. On the other hand, some government factories have reported such large losses that social costs could have hardly been less than value of output.[21] The underemployment argument for tariffs and subsidies does not hold where imported materials and equipment are a high part of total costs.

Infant-industry growth is of course a possible gain to come from either tariff or subsidy. In the long run the added efficiency won through experience may outweigh initial rises in cost and losses of income. But, as economists have long pointed out, the infant-industry argument mentions only possibilities, not certainties. Policymakers who have appealed to it usually have been too optimistic. The greater the lapse of time before the hoped-for fall in costs, the weaker is the argument for protection. Ceylon's small markets and shortage of enterprise are not the best conditions for an infant industry's growth.

PROMOTIONAL AND REDISTRIBUTIONAL POLICIES

Restrictionist policies were intended also to be promotional, to increase domestic output and encourage Ceylonese enterprise at the same time that they kept out imports and foreign firms. Certain other policies were more nearly exclusively promotional: e.g., Dry Zone colonization, village expansion, construction of government factories, research and loan assistance for local firms, the provision of "social overheads." These policies also were, in a sense, results of nationalism. Chapter 2 has pointed out how desire for economic growth was tied to the desire for "national economic independence." But the policies obviously had other as well as nationalist aspects. "Economic development" and higher incomes were viewed as goods

[21] Moreover, "real" or "social" value of output could not have exceeded the price at which equally satisfactory imports would have been available in the absence of tariffs, exchange controls, and quotas. For the record of Ceylonese government factories through 1950, see *Report of the Commission on Government Commercial Undertakings*.

per se as well as advances along the road to national freedom. Moreover, the precise forms which policy-makers (or their critics) wished economic development to take depended in part on the general social philosophies held—plus those more narrowly political considerations which influence statutes and administrative decisions in all countries. National economic independence and a higher national income were not the only policy goals.

The effects on income of promotional policies are not easy to analyze, largely because of the same difficulties that beset analysis of restrictionist policies. What part of the accounting cost charged against agricultural, industrial, and other output did not represent true social cost because the resources employed would not, in alternative employments, have contributed value equal to their recorded accounting cost to national output? What part of the accounting value attributed to output did not represent true social value because Ceylon could have imported the goods at a lower price?[22] What capital value should be assigned for favorable changes which the projects brought about in skills and attitudes significant for future production? Since Ceylon apparently suffered from mass underemployment during much of the period studied, discrepancies between accounting and social cost could have been sizable. In all those industries where tariffs, quotas, and other devices limited imports, gaps between accounting and social value were inevitable. Infant-industry gains in skills and attitudes could have occurred anywhere and redounded to the future benefit of the economy.

If the question is merely whether policy has increased income, the agricultural-expansion program is perhaps the easiest to judge. The postwar increase in paddy production is largely attributable to government policy and is clearly a net addition to national output. Higher yields in the agricultural areas have cost very little in the form of resources diverted from other uses. Similarly, although government outlays have been high, newly cultivated areas have largely been opened and worked with labor not needed to maintain

---

[22] The terms "social cost" and "social value," as employed throughout the chapter, do not have the broader connotations that sometimes characterize them in evaluations of economic behavior. The only discrepancy between "social cost" and accounting cost considered here is that attributable to the alternative unemployment or underemployment of the resources utilized; the only discrepancy between "social value" and price is that represented by the margin between price and potential import price.

the level of economic activity in the old areas. Foreign-exchange costs per unit of output have been low.

Whether a smaller outlay on colonization could not have achieved the same results is a different question. In retrospect, it seems that such was possible. The subsidies paid to colonists have been widely questioned, and the International Bank Mission argued that progress would have been more rapid if there had been less emphasis on peasant agriculture.[23] This latter, of course, points to a possible clash between the goals of agricultural expansion and social reform.

Whether a colonization program was the best possible use of available resources is still a third question, one which only a person who is quite familiar with the dynamics of Ceylonese society is fitted to answer. Some critics have argued that thoroughgoing land reform in the older areas would have permitted the introduction of intensive techniques which would have yielded a greater total return than the movement of Wet Zone peasants to the Dry Zone.[24] Problems involved here include not only the political and administrative difficulties of accomplishing the land reform, but also the task of persuading peasant farmers to depart from time-honored practices and employ the more intensive—and more onerous—techniques.

Other critics have urged that the government could have profitably diverted a large part of the colonization resources into an expanded industrial program.[25] Because of Ceylon's industrial record and because of the different requirements of agricultural and industrial production, this argument is not persuasive. On the whole, industrial policy has been much less successful than agricultural. During most years when the government has wished primarily to stimulate private manufacturing enterprise, private investors have only haltingly responded; the U. N. P.'s post-1954 policy appears to have achieved somewhat better, but still not satisfactory, results. Most of the factories which the government has itself constructed have shown such heavy accounting losses, and foreign-exchange costs have been such a large part of the total, that social cost of their output has probably exceeded its social value. The state factories

[23] International Bank Mission, *op. cit.*, pp. 388-94.

[24] E.g., E. B. Tisseverasinghe, "The Pattern of Occupation in Idealized Ceylon," *New Lanka*, VI (Jan., 1955), 53.

[25] E. g., N. K. Sarkar, "Demography of Ceylon in the Twentieth Century." But Sarkar's thesis rests in part upon his belief that urbanization is the most promising route to a lower birth rate.

which have amassed a poor record include not only the improvised wartime plants, which were mostly scrapped some years ago, but also several plants more recently constructed and still under construction. Among the weaknesses pointed out have been poorly chosen location, faulty layout and structure, and labor productivity well below that in roughly comparable Indian and privately operated Ceylonese factories.[26]

Better planning and a less political, less rule-bound system of governmental management would probably have yielded considerably better results.[27] If private enterprise had been more venturesome, assumed more of the industrial risks which government took upon itself, productivity would very likely have been still higher. The present character of the Ceylon economy, however, does not seem to be fitted for rapid industrialization, although, if "lack of enterprise" were no longer an obstacle, manufacturing might well grow much faster than it has in the recent past. Besides lack of enterprise and lack of capital, there are several other well-advertised obstacles.

One of the most important lacks is that of experienced managers and technicians, who are expensive and not familiar with local conditions if imported from abroad.[28] Another is that of suitable factory labor. Although underemployment is a major problem, Ceylon does not have a surplus of skilled workers or even of unskilled workers reasonably accustomed to the industrial discipline. Other hindrances are the comparatively high costs of importing industrial equipment and needed materials and fuel. Foreign exchange costs are, for most industrial projects, relatively high.

Finally, Ceylon's small domestic market for most manufactures means that, unless they can profitably export, many industries cannot sell in sufficient volume to achieve economies of scale for even one factory. For most potential new Ceylonese industries, export is out of the question; they could compete with imports only if

[26] See International Bank Mission, op. cit., chap. xv; and the news story on the Japanese investigating commission's report in the Ceylon Daily News, Aug. 19, 1955, "Economic Supplement."

[27] The change from departmental to semi-independent corporate management is expected to result in greater efficiency. For the reasoning involved, see Report of the Commission on Government Commercial Undertakings.

[28] For Ceylonese statements of why Western production engineers may not select what for Ceylon would be the optimum technical combinations, see the Six-Year Programme of Investment, pp. 472-74; also E. B. Tisseverasinghe, "The Content of Employment in Industry," New Lanka, VI (April, 1955), 36-43.

protected. Thus local production would add to national income only if the social cost attributable to the local resources used were very low or if the production's educational value were very high.

Promotional policies other than those in agriculture and industry have included the provision of "social overheads": e.g., roads, electric power, schools, and medical services. Except in the case of electric power, the expected return does not take the form of monetary receipts. As in other countries, there is no accounting procedure whereby benefits can be precisely calculated. Postcolonial governments have stressed that their road-improvement program has been largely concentrated in peasant areas to ease and encourage trade between nonexport agriculture and the urban sector. Schools, hospitals, and dispensaries have contributed services which have been valued highly for their direct contributions to welfare and which have helped to create conditions of progress by producing a better educated and healthier population.

But if increased productivity through better education and better health had alone been the government's goal, the educational and medical outlays probably would have to be judged too large. The number of secondary-school graduates has increased more rapidly than the economy has required their services. There has been a surplus of simple white-collar, while a shortage of technical and managerial skills.[29] Free medical aid has, because of is very merits, produced further population increase in an overcrowded land where much labor is already largely idle. Much of the capital and energy poured into the educational and medical programs could probably have increased "output" more if invested in "productive capacity." In so far as its past contribution is concerned, much the same can be said of the hydroelectric project, which was launched in the 1920's to revolutionize Ceylon's economy, but which did not contribute electric light and power before 1950 and which has not yet played a major industrial role.

In all those instances, agricultural, industrial, and "social overhead," where accounting cost exceeded social value of output, government policy brought about a redistribution of income within Ceylon, whether or not the policy increased aggregate income. Taxes

[29] See E. B. Tisseverasinghe, "The Pattern of Occupation in Idealized Ceylon," *New Lanka*, VI (Jan., 1955), 51.

and price rises caused by taxes or import restrictions took income away; subsidies and prices in excess of social contributions redistributed it. To the extent that the added taxes and price rises hit foreign residents and absentee owners, the redistribution of course added to aggregate Ceylonese income; but the bulk of the income transfer must have occurred among the Ceylonese themselves. Groups benefiting from such redistribution include colonists, peasants in areas where population pressure was relieved, factory employees, and investors protected from foreign competition. Injured groups included urban consumers and those whose taxes were increased because of the subsidies and the state factories' losses; most of the added taxes presumably came from upper-income pockets.

Goods and services which the government has provided without charge or at a price below cost, together with the taxes and budgetary deficits employed to pay for them, have formed another and more substantial means of redistribution. Benefits here have included the road, school, and health services mentioned above plus subsidized rice and, for a few years, very modest midday meals for school children. Obviously, there is no way of knowing precisely what taxes would have been lower had the government not provided these benefits, but very probably the ratio of services received to taxes contributed was high for the lower-income brackets, low for the upper-income brackets. Government profits on imported sugar provided part of the needed revenues. Import restrictions passed another part of the burden on to urban and other consumers, especially those with above-average incomes.

Again, some income must have been transferred from foreign residents and absentee owners to Ceylonese. Nor was this the only nationalist aspect of the redistributional program. Observed discrepancies between local and foreign incomes have produced a desire not only to tax the outsider, but also to provide the Ceylonese masses with opportunities and services more nearly comparable with those enjoyed abroad. Nationalist pride, as well as egalitarian sentiment and hopes for progress through improved education and health, has demanded free schools and hospitals for Ceylon.

From one standpoint, however, the principal redistribution achieved was not that between different groups, but rather that between capital formation and consumption. The government drew down foreign balances to enable it to maintain its welfare program, and probably reduced its rupee capital outlay as well. To the extent that the welfare expenditures increased the nation's ability to produce, they also added to effective capital; but, as has been stated above, probably much of the outlay on education and health did not have this effect. The rice subsidy probably added very little to production potentialities.

The high taxes which Ceylon imposed must also have depressed capital formation by decreasing the incentive to invest. But the diminution caused in this way may not have been very large. Private enterprise was not very venturesome when income taxes were much lower. To the extent that the taxes substituted governmental investment for consumption and the speculative bidding up of land values,[30] they obviously brought about a rise in the nation's capital.

SUMMARY AND CONCLUSIONS

What, then, can be said in conclusion about the effects which nationalist sentiment and government policies have had upon Ceylonese incomes? The picture is cloudy and complicated; social costs, infant-industry gains, and social overheads' contributions are all impossible to calculate. It appears that nationalist sentiment has raised income only through its favorable effects upon Ceylonese ambitions and efforts. Restrictionist policies which nationalism has demanded probably have on balance lowered Ceylonese incomes somewhat, and foreign investors' fears of an uncertain future have been distinctly unfavorable for the island's economic advance. The government's industrial ventures have not to date amassed an impressive record, but the questions of social costs and possible infant-industry gains are especially tricky. Agricultural ventures must have substantially added to national income, but a somewhat different allocation of the resources employed may well have added more. The contributions assigned to education and health depend upon the values assigned to these as goods in themselves. Promotional, restrictionist, and fiscal policies have redistributed income, apparently in large part from higher to lower brackets. Heavy welfare expenditures have slowed capital formation, and high taxes must have played a similar although perhaps much less important role.

[30] See *Report of the Committee on Utilization of Crown Lands*, pp. 10-12; Jennings, *The Economy of Ceylon*, pp. 33-35.

Most of these estimates are highly conditional. Many, perhaps most, Ceylonese do not accept them, even in this conditional form. Moreover, even if less conditional estimates were possible, and if they were so firmly established that no one would disagree, they still would not provide an adequate summing up of all effects in which the Ceylonese are interested, since the Ceylonese do not regard level and distribution of income as the only important criteria of economic policy. Those orators and writers who praise national economic independence may believe that a move toward independence brings economic gain, but they also treasure it for its own sake. The more fervent nationalists would pay a high price if they could thereby substitute Ceylonese for foreign owners, managers, and workers, and make the Ceylonese economy less dependent on imports and Western markets.

SELECTED BIBLIOGRAPHY

The bibliography suggested here includes Ceylonese and Western books and articles and Ceylon Government publications dealing with Ceylonese economic, political, and certain sociological questions. Unfortunately, Ceylonese journals and government publications are not generally available in Western libraries.

The Preface and footnotes provide a lengthier list of Ceylonese writings.

Government and History

BOOKS

BAILEY, S. D. *Ceylon.* New York: Hutchinson's University Library, 1952.

COLLINS, SIR CHARLES HENRY. *Public Administration in Ceylon.* London and New York: Royal Institute of International Affairs, 1951.

HOLDEN, LORD ANGUS. *Ceylon.* London: G. Allen and Unwin, Ltd., 1939.

JENNINGS, SIR WILLIAM IVOR. *The Constitution of Ceylon.* Bombay and New York: Oxford University Press, 1951.

JENNINGS, SIR IVOR, AND TAMBIAH, H. W. *The Dominion of Ceylon: The Development of Its Laws and Constitution.* London: George Stevens and Sons, 1952.

JENNINGS, SIR IVOR. *Nationalism and Political Development in Ceylon,* New York: Institute of Pacific Relations, 1950.

KOTELAWALA, SIR JOHN. *An Asian Prime Minister's Story.* London: George G. Harrap and Co., 1956.

MENDIS, G. C. *Ceylon under the British.* Colombo: Apothecaries Press, 1952.

NAMASIVAYAM, S.   *The Legislatures of Ceylon, 1928-48.*   London: Faber and Faber, 1951.

WEERAWARDANA, I. D. S. *Government and Politics in Ceylon, 1931-46.* Colombo: Ceylon Research Associates, 1951.

WEERAWARDANA, I. D. S.   *The Senate of Ceylon at Work.*   Colombo: University of Ceylon Press, 1955.

WEERAWARDANA, I. D. S. AND WEERAWARDANA, M. I. *Ceylon and Her Citizens.* Madras: Oxford University Press, 1956.

ARTICLES IN CEYLONESE JOURNALS

JENNINGS, W. IVOR.   "The Appointment of the Soulbury Commission," *University of Ceylon Review,* III (Nov., 1945), 11-28.

JENNINGS, W. IVOR.   "The Evolution of the New Constitution," *University of Ceylon Review,* V (April, 1947), 1-16.

JENNINGS, W. IVOR.   "The Ceylon General Election of 1947," *University of Ceylon Review,* VI (July, 1948), 133-95.

JENNINGS, SIR IVOR.   "Nationalism and Political Development in Ceylon," *Ceylon Historical Journal,* III (July, 1953), 62-85; III (Oct. 1953), 99-114; III (Jan.-April, 1954), 197-206.

KURUPPU, N. S. G.   "A History of the Working-Class Movement in Ceylon: I—Labour and the Rise of Capitalism: An Outline to the Year 1935," *Ceylon Historical Journal,* I (Oct., 1951), 129-46.

MENDIS, G. C.   "The Causes of Communal Conflict in Ceylon," *University of Ceylon Review,* I (April, 1943), 41-49.

MENDIS, G. C.   "Adult Franchise and Educational Reform," *University of Ceylon Review,* II (Nov., 1944), 37-44.

NAGULESWARAN, P.   "A History of the Working-Class Movement in Ceylon: II—The Problem of Indian Immigrant Labour in the Nineteenth Century," *Ceylon Historical Journal,* I (Jan., 1952), 230-41.

PASSÉ, H. A.   "The English Language in Ceylon," *University of Ceylon Review,* I (Nov., 1943), 50-65.

PIERIS, RALPH.   "Society and Ideology in Ceylon during a 'Time of Troubles,' 1795-1850," *University of Ceylon Review,* IX (July, 1951), 171-185; IX (Oct., 1951), 266-79; X (Jan., 1952), 79-102.

VANDEN DRIESEN, I.   "The History of Coffee Culture in Ceylon," *Ceylon Historical Journal,* III (July, 1953), 31-61; III (Oct., 1953), 156-72.

WEERAWARDANA, I. D. S.   "The Minorities and the Citizenship Act," *Ceylon Historical Journal,* I (Jan., 1952), 242-50.

WEERAWARDANA, I. D. S. "The General Elections in Ceylon, 1952," *Ceylon Historical Journal*, II (July-Oct., 1952), 109-78.

ARTICLES IN OTHER JOURNALS

"A 'People's Government': Social and Political Trends in Ceylon," *World Today*, July, 1956, pp. 281-91.

JENNINGS, W. I. "Ceylon's 1952 Election," *Far Eastern Survey*, XXI (Dec. 3, 1952), 177-80.

JENNINGS, SIR IVOR. "Politics in Ceylon since 1952," *Pacific Affairs*, XXVII (Dec., 1954), 338-52.

WEERAWARDANA, I. D. S. "Minority Problems in Ceylon," *Pacific Affairs*, XXV (Sept., 1952), 278-87.

Geography and Sociology

BOOKS

COOK, ELSIE K. *Ceylon: Its Geography, Its Resources and Its People.* Madras: Macmillan, 1951.

RYAN, BRYCE. *Caste in Modern Ceylon.* New Brunswick, N. J.; Rutgers University Press, 1953.

WIJESEKERA, N. D. *The People of Ceylon.* Colombo: M.D. Gunasena and Co., 1950.

ARTICLES IN CEYLONESE JOURNALS

GREEN, T. L. "Education and Social Needs in Ceylon," *University of Ceylon Review*, I (Oct., 1952), 297-316.

JENNINGS, W. IVOR. "Race, Religion and Economic Opportunity in the University of Ceylon," *University of Ceylon Review*, II (Nov., 1944), 1-13.

MACFADDEN, C. H. "The Geographical Basis for Ceylon's National Planning," *University of Ceylon Review*, IX (Oct., 1951), 252-59.

MENDIS, G. C. "The Causes of Communal Conflict in Ceylon," *University of Ceylon Review*, I (April, 1943), 41-49.

MENDIS, G. C. "Adult Franchise and Educational Reform," *University of Ceylon Review*, II (Nov., 1944), 37-44.

PASSÉ, H. A. "The English Language in Ceylon," *University of Ceylon Review*, I (Nov., 1943), 50-65.

PIERIS, RALPH. "Society and Ideology in Ceylon during a 'Time of Troubles,' 1795-1850," *University of Ceylon Review*, IX (July, 1951), 171-85; IX (Oct., 1951), 266-79; X (Jan., 1952), 79-102.

SENANAYAKE, D. S.   "The Qualities Required of Public Servants," *University of Ceylon Review*, VI (Jan., 1948), 1-6.

STRAUSS, MURRAY A.   "Family Characteristics and Occupational Choice of University Entrants as Clues to the Social Structure of Ceylon," *University of Ceylon Review*, IX (April, 1951), 125-35.

ARTICLES IN OTHER JOURNALS

RYAN, BRYCE.   "The Ceylonese Village and the New Value System," *Rural Sociology*, XVII (March, 1952), 9-28.

RYAN, BRYCE.   "West and East in Ceylon," *Journal of Educational Sociology*, XXVI (April, 1953), 342-55.

RYAN, BRYCE, AND STRAUSS, MURRAY A.   "The Integration of Sinhalese Society," *Research Studies of the State College of Washington*, XXII (Dec., 1954), 179-227.

STRAUSS, MURRAY A.   "Cultural Factors in the Functioning of Agricultural Extension in Ceylon," *Rural Sociology*, XVIII (Sept., 1953), 249-56.

STRAUSS, MURRAY A.   "Subcultural Variation in Ceylonese Mental Ability: A Study in National Character," *Journal of Social Psychology*, XXXIX, First Half (Feb., 1954), 129-141.

Economic Conditions, Policies and Problems

BOOKS

CRANE, ROBERT I.   *Aspects of Economic Development in South Asia,* with a Supplement on *Development Problems in Ceylon* by Burton Stein.   New York: Institute of Pacific Relations, 1954.

INTERNATIONAL BANK OF RECONSTRUCTION AND DEVELOPMENT.   *The Economic Development of Ceylon.*   Baltimore: Johns Hopkins Press, 1953.

JENNINGS, SIR IVOR.   *The Economy of Ceylon.*   Madras: Oxford University Press, 1951.

SHENOY, B. R.   *Ceylon Currency and Banking.*   London: Longmans, Green & Co., 1941.

ARTICLES IN CEYLONESE JOURNALS: PRE-1947

BRAYNE, C. V.   "The Problem of Peasant Agriculture in Ceylon," *Ceylon Economic Journal*, Dec., 1934, pp. 34-46.

DAS GUPTA, B. B.   "Local Authorities and Housing in Ceylon," *University of Ceylon Review*, II (Nov., 1944), 68-76.

DAS GUPTA, B. B.   "The Slump in Staples," *Ceylon Economic Journal*, Dec., 1932, pp. 44-59.

FERNANDO, SIR H. MARCUS. "On the Banking and Other Credit Facilities in Ceylon," *Ceylon Economic Journal,* Dec., 1931, pp. 1-13.

GUHA, K. D.. "Certain Aspects of Industrial Planning in Ceylon," *Ceylon Economic Journal,* Dec., 1937, pp. 57-64.

DAS GUPTA, B. B. "Rural Economic Data from Kalutara District," *Ceylon Economic Journal,* Dec., 1937, pp. 65-79.

MENON, K. P. S. "Indian Labour in Ceylon," *Ceylon Economic Journal,* Dec., 1932, pp. 1-17.

OBEYSEKERE, DANTON G. "Random Thoughts on the National Income of Ceylon," *Ceylon Economic Journal,* Dec., 1946, pp. 39-55.

SENEVIRATNE, L. J. DE S. "Land Tenure in the Kandyan Provinces," *Ceylon Economic Journal,* Dec., 1937, pp. 35-56.

ARTICLES IN CEYLONESE JOURNALS: POST-1947

COREA, GAMANI. "Some Problems of Economic Development in Ceylon," *Ceylon Economist,* I (Aug., 1950), 39-54.

DAS GUPTA, B. B. "International Commodity Arrangements and Ceylon," *Ceylon Economist,* I (Feb., 1951), 223-29.

DAS GUPTA, B. B. "The Theory and Reality of Economic Development," *Central Bank of Ceylon Bulletin,* Nov., 1955, pp. 10-14.

GUNASEKERA, H. A. DE S. "Thoughts on Full Employment," *Ceylon Economist,* I (Nov., 1950), 191-98.

JAYAWARDENA, N. U. "The Problem of Liquidity in Under-Developed Countries," *Ceylon Economist,* II (Second Quarter, 1952), 93-101.

KELEGAMA, J. B. "The Kandyan Peasantry Problem," *Ceylon Economist,* II (Third Quarter, 1952), 181-93; II (July, 1953), 264-76.

KULURATNAM, K. "Minerals and the Economic Development of Ceylon," *Ceylon Economist,* III (Sept., 1954), 11-26.

LEEMBRUGGEN, J. A. "Exchange Control in Ceylon," *Ceylon Economist,* I (June, 1951), 375-86.

RASAPUTRAM, W. "Inflation in Ceylon," *Ceylon Economist,* I (June, 1951), 322-30.

RUPESINGHE, W. "The Paddy Lands Bill," *Ceylon Economist,* II (July, 1953), 277-85.

SARKAR, N. K. "The First Year of the Central Bank," *Ceylon Economist,* I (June, 1951), 315-21.

SENEWIRATNE, S. T. "A Study of the Gal Oya Project," *Ceylon Economist,* II (Sept., 1951), 69-76.

SIRIWARDENE, D. R. "The External Value of the Ceylon Rupee," *Ceylon Economist,* II (Sept., 1951), 40-50.

TISSEVERASINGHE, E. B. "The Scope of Small Industry in Ceylon,"
  New Lanka, VI (Oct., 1954), 25-31.
TISSEVERASINGHE, E. B. "The Pattern of Occupation in Idealized Cey-
  lon," *New Lanka,* VI (Jan., 1955), 47-59.
TISSEVERASINGHE, E. B. "The Content of Employment in Industry,"
  New Lanka, VI (April, 1955), 36-43.
WADINAMBIARATCHI, G. H. "Postscript to Devaluation," *Ceylon Econ-
  omist,* II (Third Quarter, 1952), 200-206.

ARTICLES IN OTHER JOURNALS

"Development Planning in Ceylon," *International Labor Review,*
  LXXIII (Feb., 1956), 194-209.
ELLSWORTH, P. T. "Factors in the Economic Development of Ceylon,"
  American Economic Review, XLIII (May, 1953), 115-25.
FARMER, B. H. "Agriculture in Ceylon," *Geographical Review,* XL
  (Jan., 1950), 42-66.
FARMER, B. H. "Peasant Colonization in Ceylon," *Pacific Affairs,* XXV
  (Dec., 1952), 387-398.
MORGAN, THEODORE, "The Economic Development of Ceylon,"
  Annals of the American Academy of Political and Social Science,
  CCCV (May, 1956), 92-100.
MORGAN, THEODORE. "Distribution of Income in Ceylon, Puerto Rico,
  the United States and the United Kingdom," *Economic Journal,*
  LXIII (Dec., 1953), 821-34.
REID, MARGARET G. "Survey of Ceylon's Consumer Finances," *Ameri-
  can Economic Review,* XLVI (Dec., 1956), 956-964.

Ceylon Government Publications

LEGISLATIVE COUNCIL: COLONIAL GOVERNMENT

*Papers relating to the Development of the Economic Resources of the
  Colony* (Sessional Paper VI, 1921)
Report of the Industries Commission (Sessional Paper I, 1922)
Report of the Special Commission on the Ceylon Constitution (Colombo:
  Government Printer, 1928)

STATE COUNCIL: SEMI-AUTONOMY

*Dispatches from the Secretary of State for the Colonies regarding the
  Development of the Co-operative Movement in the Colonial De-
  pendencies* (Sessional Paper I, 1947)
First Interim Report of the Technical Adviser on Industries (Sessional
  Paper XV, 1935)

New State-Owned Factories (Sessional Paper XXIII, 1947)

Postwar Development Proposals (Government Record Office, 1946)

Report of the Ceylon Banking Commission (Sessional Paper XXII, 1934)

Report of the Commission on Social Services (Sessional Paper VII, 1947)

Report of the Commission on Constitutional Reform (London: His Majesty's Stationery Office, September, 1945, Cmd. 6677)

Report on Industrial Development and Policy (Sessional Paper XV, 1946)

Report on the Proposal to Introduce Statutory Provision for Poor Relief in Ceylon (Sessional Paper XX, 1934)

Report on Rural Reconstruction in Ceylon (Sessional Paper XXIII, 1944)

PARLIAMENT: INDEPENDENCE

Census of Ceylon, 1946

Census of Agriculture, 1952

Census of Industry, 1952

Ceylon Year Book (1949-   )

Statistical Abstract of Ceylon (1951-   )

Administration Report of the Acting Director of Industries for the Years 1940-1947 (December, 1951)

Economic and Social Development of Ceylon (a Survey), 1926-1954 (Ministry of Finance, July 1, 1955)

Final Report on the Economic Survey of Rural Ceylon (Sessional Paper XI, 1954)

Report of the Commission on Government Commercial Undertakings (Sessional Paper XIX, 1953)

Report of the Committee on Utilization of Crown Lands (Sessional Paper III, 1953)

Report of the Kandyan Peasantry Commission (Sessional Paper XVIII, 1951)

Report of the Taxation Commission (Sessional Paper XVII, 1955)

Report on the Survey of Landlessness (Sessional Paper XIII, 1952)

Six-Year Programme of Investment, 1954-55 to 1959-60 (Planning Secretariat, 1955)

Six-Year Plan for Ceylon (Department of Information, 1950)

Survey of Ceylon's Consumer Finances (Central Bank of Ceylon, 1954)

INDEX